You

Can

Share the Faith

You
Can
Share the Faith:

REACHING OUT
ONE PERSON
AT A TIME

Karen Edmisten

Our Sunday Visitor Publishing Division
Our Sunday Visitor, Inc.
Huntington, Indiana 46750

Copyright © 2016 by Karen Edmisten. Published 2016

21 20 19 18 17 16   1 2 3 4 5 6 7 8 9

Our Sunday Visitor Publishing Division
Our Sunday Visitor, Inc.
200 Noll Plaza
Huntington, IN 46750
1-800-348-2440

ISBN: 978-1-61278-913-2 (Inventory No. T1696)
eISBN: 978-1-61278-919-4
LCCN: 2015958295

Cover design: Lindsey Riesen
Cover art: Shutterstock
Interior design: Dianne Nelson

PRINTED IN THE UNITED STATES OF AMERICA

Dedication

For Emily, Lizzy, and Katy,
who have shared Jesus with me
in ways untold.

Contents

Introduction

I HAVE A CONFESSION. When I hear the Scripture verse about going forth and making disciples of all nations, I want to run and hide. *All* nations? That's a lot of people. I feel defeated before I've begun. I'm itching to spread the Good News, but I don't think I know how to spread it that far and wide.

Global coverage sounds daunting. It conjures up images of tromping town to town and country to country. It sounds as if we're all required to be missionaries in this manner. But is that true? What does evangelization look like on a practical level?

Since Jesus was the first and best at it, we should follow his lead. He started small, asking Peter, "Join me?" Peter said yes. Then Jesus invited Peter's brother, Andrew, to come along. A handful of guys here, a couple more there, and in no time Jesus had an active band of followers. This premiere Christian evangelization was carried out quietly—except on those occasions when they jostled for position—and without fanfare. But this humble start bore tremendous fruit, thanks to the Leader, who knew the importance of interpersonal communication.

Fast-forward to the twenty-first century. There are efforts at evangelization all around us. Parish initiatives, programs, books (like this one), lectures, conferences. Everywhere a concerned Christian looks he's faced with the problem of the century ("How do we spread the Gospel?") and proposed solutions ("How to spread the Gospel in five easy steps!")

On the flip side are the intended targets of this evangelization. Poor targets. They must wonder who left the would-be missionaries in charge. The seeming presumption of a missionary is disconcerting at best and maddening at worst in a world that believes we each create our own truth. "Who are you to tell me your way is best?" the skeptic asks. "What right do you have to foist your beliefs on me?" wonders the agnostic, the atheist, the cynic, and the seeker. Those are excellent questions, worth asking. Why *not* question evangelists? With so many worldviews clamoring for humanity's attention, which belief system should one adopt, which voice does one heed?

The gut reaction of a genuine Christian evangelist is that he isn't trying to foist God on anyone. His goal is not coercion or a demand that everyone line up and become carbon copies of his admirable, Trinitarian-believing self. An authentic evangelist is far more interested in the very real person who's sitting next to him, talking about last night's thunderstorm or the Pixar movie he took his kids to see last week. He cares more about living, breathing, messy human beings than about fashioning religious clones. The evangelist chooses meaningful discussion over clever, well-timed lectures. In short, the evangelist shares his life—the spiritual life that Jesus Christ gave him.

That evangelist, simply put, is you and I. We are already evangelizing when we chat with friends, keep a neighbor company, and dig into the stuff of this world—mundane daily tasks, humble little jobs, or huge, sobering responsibilities. It's happening when we catch up with coworkers on Monday morning or offer quiet intercessory prayer on Friday night. It happens when we befriend people from all walks of life, not because our goal is to mass-produce spiritual copies, but because we have found something incredible—life in Jesus Christ—and we want to share it with everyone we know. So we talk about what we've found, this thing that is worthy of sharing. We can't *help* but share it.

These facets of evangelism—components of friendship and respect, really—say, "There's something out there that's bigger than we are, and Someone who cares about us, who wants us to band together." When we lose a job, have a baby, investigate nursing homes for our parents, Someone is there. When we cradle a broken heart, are deployed, are left behind during deployment, volunteer at a homeless shelter, go to the movies, discuss Nietzsche, are ill, or become victims of violence, Someone is there. When we pray in a cold church on a Tuesday afternoon, wondering if anyone hears us, Someone is there. Someone who knows and cares about every detail of our lives, right down to the pattern of the socks we're wearing, and why we couldn't sleep last night.

When we see that truth, we know there's no presumption in being an evangelist. It is a way of life. Like any life, it can be tiring, exciting, joyful, discouraging, and sometimes overwhelming, but the one thing it's not is presumptuous. How can it be presumptuous to know you were given the gift of never-ending nourishment and, in return, hope you can help feed a hungry world?

Pope Francis said: "The Lord's relationship with his people is a personal relationship, always. It is a person-to-person relationship.... It is not a dialogue between the Almighty and the masses."[1] Christianity is an incarnational faith. Jesus Christ came to us with flesh, blood, sweat, and tears, and he continues to work that way. Person to person, one soul, one friendship at a time. Jesus never forced himself on anyone, and we don't have to, either. Jesus worked, loved, discussed, went to parties, prayed, asked for wine, slept when he was tired, and talked about his Father. He invited. He invites us to do the same.

This book, then, is about such invitations. It's about people like you and me and their sometimes amazing yet ordinary examples of what it means to be a witness for Jesus Christ. It's about the beauty of the missionary spirit in action. It is about relationship, with God and with each other.

You might ask: "But who is this book for? Is this about evangelizing non-Catholics? Fallen-away Catholics? Other religions, agnostics, or atheists? Or me?"

Yes. We're all called to evangelize, and we all need ongoing evangelization. St. Francis of Assisi said that if we sanctified ourselves we'd sanctify society. It's a never-ending process, but a simple one. There's really only one "Do" and one "Don't" when it comes to sharing the faith: Do live your love for Jesus and share it, person to person, one relationship at a time. Don't ever give up on anyone, because you never know what God is doing behind the veil.

Far from daunting, making disciples is exhilarating. Just do as Jesus did: start small. One person. The Holy Spirit, whom Pope Francis calls the "witness of Jesus who tells us where Jesus is, how to find Jesus, what Jesus tells us,"[2] will do the heavy lifting.

Go forth.

CHAPTER 1

Do Remember That
You're Being Watched

I GREW UP WITHOUT GOD.

That sounds nihilistic, but it wasn't that dramatic. We didn't denounce nattily dressed neighbors who scurried off to church, or throw rocks through local stained-glass windows. There was nothing rebellious or ugly, just a houseful of souls muddling through life, trying to figure it all out. We spent Sunday mornings as a family, with dad's famous animal-shaped pancakes, or mom's French toast, or brunch at the Officers' Club on special occasions. My father was an Air Force pilot and we moved every couple of years, meeting and befriending diverse families. My childhood was populated with kind, loving, interesting people. It just didn't happen to be populated by God.

We did have some of the cultural trappings of Christianity. Naturally, we always had a Christmas tree, who didn't? There were glittery stockings and gifts galore. Santa's visits to our house on Christmas Eve made me a huge fan of the holiday. It was magical. At Easter, I looked forward to chocolate bunnies piled high in a pastel basket—a beloved family tradition, and who doesn't love a good Easter egg hunt? My household may not have believed in God, but we believed in love and family. However, when the Christmas decorations were packed away and all the Easter candy consumed, we moved on, unchanged.

There are millions of households in the United States like ours was. Good, kind people who live their lives somewhere in the agnostic-to-atheist realm because they've never really been introduced to Christianity. My parents were and are—I'm blessed to still have them—kind, decent, wonderful people whom I love very much. They are children of God, and I'm certain he's quite fond of them. When I think of my parents, or of myself in the days before my conversion, my husband before his, or any number of people I know, I remember a quote from Garrison Keillor. He said somewhere, of a friend, that although she doesn't believe in God there's evidence that God believes in her. I think God believes in all of us, and he'd like us to be conduits of the evidence.

My childhood home was a lovely place to grow up, and I was well loved and cared for. But because we didn't talk about God, I felt no pressing need to search for him. In reality, of course, God was always right next to me, but when you've grown up as I did—and as my parents did before me, and their parents before them—unbaptized and uncatechized, what *does* spark an interest in him? What would make a girl raised in a secular home even begin to care?

Though I didn't realize it as I was growing up, I watched believers. Subconsciously, I recorded the actions, behaviors, and sincerity (or lack of it) of those who professed belief in Jesus Christ. The witness of Christians, for good or ill, left a deep imprint on my psyche, forming my ideas about Christianity.

Being Nothing

My earliest memory of organized religion is of a Sunday school classroom: paper dolls dressed in robes and sandals, and me, at a loss as to what to do with them. A teacher who seemed unwelcoming, unengaged. I remember only sitting alone that day. The visitor, the stranger. A few years ago, I asked my parents about the experience, and they said they tried going to church once or twice but didn't continue.

Religion didn't come up again until junior high school. A break in French class found a few of us sitting around chatting. Someone asked what religion everyone's family was. Classmates around the circle confidently ticked off their answers. Catholic! Methodist! Baptist!

I panicked. Clearly, everyone was something, but what was I? I didn't have an answer to that question. It had never seemed particularly important, and no one had ever asked me before. I vaguely perceived that Christians were divided into two big camps: Catholics and Protestants. I knew we weren't Catholic, because *those* people were really strange and extreme. Were we *some* kind of Christian? We celebrated Christmas, right? And Easter. We must be something.

"Umm, we're Protestant," I mumbled, when my turn came around.

"Yeah, but what *kind*?" someone persisted.

"I don't know," I bristled, "we're just Protestant."

"That's not how it works," someone muttered in disgust. "You have to be *something*."

A few smirks indicated that my classmates were unimpressed with my lack of religious clarity. It was the first time I genuinely grasped that my family and I were "nothing."

My next encounter with religion came when my friend Cathy started dropping notes in my locker. "Jesus loves you," the notes said. I was irritated. Cathy and I had never talked about religion, so why was she bringing it up now? Didn't she know I was officially "nothing"? I went with my gut reaction: I didn't know Jesus, and "love" implied too much intimacy for the nonexistent terms I was on with him. I ignored her note-dropping.

Then one day Cathy invited me out for pizza with her family. Never one to turn down anything involving pepperoni, I accepted. Cathy and her family picked me up that evening and we headed out, but not in the direction of any pizza place I knew. When we pulled into a church parking lot, I stiffened. What was going on? Cathy had not mentioned a church. What was wrong with Pizza Hut or Pizza Inn or *anyplace else that was not a church?* On high alert, I scoped out the premises as I gingerly followed Cathy and her family inside. Witnessing nothing but the conspicuous consumption of pizza, I relaxed. I had overreacted.

We ate our meal in a cafeteria-style room, and I thought, "Whew, it *is* just a social thing, it *is* just pizza." But after dinner, my initial suspicions were confirmed as the night morphed into something surreal. I didn't know the term "altar call" at the time, but I knew something entirely outside of my experience was happening. I was captive in a church, listening to a preacher exclaim, "If you accept Jesus Christ as your personal Lord and Savior, come on down!"

As I sat in the middle of this crowd, my eyes scrunched shut, something odd happened: I felt slightly drawn to the offer. Wait, what? For a fraction of a second I imagined myself responding, pictured myself running forward, as others did, weeping and gasping, "Yes! Yes!" What would happen if I did it? What if I flung myself into the wave of humanity at the front of the church?

I had to admit that the euphoria and peace they promised sounded enticing. But I didn't understand how I could automatically, magically receive such gifts. If I were going to say yes to this, I needed to understand what "this" was, how the package was to be delivered. There was no logic in the claim that my life would change overnight after running down an aisle, flailing my arms, and shouting, "Count me in, God!"

And then there was the anger. Oh, the growing, swelling anger! I seethed. Cathy lied to me. Lied to get me to her church, lied to get me into this whatever-it-was. My fury at her trickery was stronger than the flickering spark of the moment. So I sat frozen, glued to my seat until the whole thing ended. The emotion died down, the people around me drifted back to earth, and it was time to gather our things and go. I don't even remember the conversation on the way home; I closed in on myself, shut down, enshrouded in my wrath.

Cathy's family dropped me off at my front door, unconverted and defiant. They had not persuaded me of their dogma, but they had convinced me of one thing: Christians were untrustworthy fakes who lied and schemed to get you into the club. If the club was worth joining, I thought, they wouldn't resort to such pathetic recruiting tactics. I was done with them.

Fasting and Feasting

High school brought another Christian into my life. In my junior year drama class, I performed a scene from Neil Simon's *Star Spangled Girl* and my impression of a southern ingenue caught the attention of a tall, skinny boy named Jack. After class, he followed me down the hall to my next class, chattering all the way about what a great actress I was. I approved of his taste in actresses, and as it turned out we also shared a love of books, movies, and nonstop talking. In no time we were best friends. I became a permanent fixture at Jack's house for the rest of my high school career.

Jack's family was Catholic, the first Catholics I ever really got to know. Jack's mother, Loretta, was bigger than life, a Philadelphia girl who married an Air Force guy and landed in the heartland where she was completely out of place and yet somehow perfectly, exactly where she should be. I didn't realize it until years later when I learned the term, but Loretta was a corporal work of mercy in action. She befriended strays and welcomed anyone and everyone into her home. Lonely, middle-aged man? Come to dinner! Misfit teen hiding behind overgrown bangs? Get thee to the party! Priest? Join us! She threw dinner parties and holiday feasts, inviting the lonely, the gregarious, the cool and uncool, the kids who had loads of friends, and the kids who had none. And she made the best chocolate pound cake this side of Philadelphia.

Loretta had strict "Crazy Catholic Rules" as I called them: Sunday morning at the Donnelly house was for Mass, no exceptions, ever, under any circumstance. Boys and girls were not allowed behind the closed doors of a bedroom, no exceptions, ever, under any circumstance. The Donnelly kids joked that there may as well have been a Hays Code stating that if you *were* in a bedroom with a member of the opposite sex, merely sitting on a bed chatting, at least one foot per person had to be touching the floor. And Donnelly children, upon arriving home on a Saturday night, awakened their mother immediately to tell her they were home and safe. Rules were nonnegotiable. No exceptions, ever.

But if I thought these crazy, rigid Catholics had to fast from a certain amount of freedom, they also proved that Catholics knew how to feast. On the 6th of January every year—I didn't know it was called the Epiphany—the Donnelly Christmas tree was still up. My family, like *normal* people, kept our tree up until New Year's Day, but what kind of crazies kept a tree up until January 6? *Why?* I found out why. Loretta threw a Twelfth Night party. I had never heard of Twelfth Night, aside from Shakespeare, so I was curious. And what a party! Platters heavy with hot, bacon-y hors d'oeuvres, Loretta's rich chocolate pound cake, fruit punch, coffee with heavy cream, wine and Irish coffee for the adults. Sweet strains of Christmas music played against the backdrop of a twinkling, bubble-light tree.

It was magical. And it was my first exposure to countercultural religious revelry—the Catholic feasting that celebrates the entire season in a world that packs Christmas away too soon. These Catholics were a strange but intriguing bunch. I hung around them until it was time to move away for college, where I met another set of Catholics who ran the gamut from textbook cases of hypocrisy to a girl I hated for her goodness.

Hidden Pain

In my first month at college, I went to a party at someone's apartment. I wasn't used to drinking, but wanted to fit in and quickly got tipsy after two beers. I didn't like feeling fuzzy and decided to leave. One of the hosts—I'll call him Allen—encouraged me to stay. I was initially flattered by Allen's attention, but was just as immediately uncomfortable with the way he tugged me back when I tried to mingle, or pulled me next to him each time I announced I was leaving. I felt awkward, embarrassed, and didn't know how to react. Soon, the last few stragglers were filtering out the door, and I followed. But Allen tugged me back one last time. I was about to become a statistic.

All I remember of the aftermath of the assault is staggering back to my dorm, wondering how I could have been so stupid. I hated myself for not leaving the party the moment Allen made me feel uncomfortable, even scared. I wrapped my sweater around my waist to cover up the fact that my jeans had a ripped zipper and were missing a button.

Shock and denial took over. Rationally, I knew that a normal man doesn't hold a crying woman down on a bed. Normal men understand that "No!" and "Stop!" mean *no* and *stop*. But I blamed myself. *Stupid girl*, I thought. *Get a grip.*

In the following days, Allen made sure his friends knew I was an easy mark. It was confusing and unspeakably painful to hear that he'd bragged about his "conquest." I hated him, but didn't know how to stand up to him. That night would haunt me for years. Instead of facing the reality that I'd been through an actual assault that left me sinking into depression, I acted out and self-medicated, treating the problem with copious amounts of alcohol, an important detail in a discussion about conversion and sharing the faith. I was not alone in this: Girls and young women who appear to be making selfish and sinful choices are sometimes, in fact, self-destructing due to hidden pain. "Every heart," Henry Wadsworth Longfellow wrote, "has its secret sorrows, which the world knows not, and oftentimes we call a man cold, when he is only sad."[3]

I turned into a drinker almost overnight, and among my partying friends were some Catholics who didn't seem to live by the teachings of their Church. I wasn't sure why they bothered to call themselves Catholic when they didn't take their faith seriously. Though I didn't believe in God and disagreed with the Catholic Church myself, I was struck by their lack of intellectual honesty.

A Different Way to Live

Late in my freshman year, I began dating a nice Catholic boy. Early in our relationship, Jon asked me what I believed. "Nothing," I had to say. "I'm sorry." I thought he'd drop me immediately, but when one is eighteen and falling in love, such differences don't always matter. Jon was a serious Catholic who went to Mass, prayed, talked about God, got excited about the pope visiting the United States, and went to confession. That last fact confounded me because I couldn't get him to do anything that seemed confess-able. He placed firm limits on our physical relationship, boundaries I had no choice but to respect. He sacrificed personal desires and pleasure for the sake of his faith. I was stunned by his fortitude.

While I was dating Jon, I was also friends with Stephen, another Catholic. Stephen was a quintessential "old soul." Although he was only a couple years older than the rest of us in the theater department, he was a grandfather figure. He took an interest in everyone's well-being, chided those who didn't passionately throw everything into "our work" (theater majors can be grandiose), and doled out advice on a regular basis.

Sometimes over coffee, Stephen soliloquized to me in subdued, mystical tones about God and about the future of my relationship with Jon. Peering over the tops of his glasses, Stephen assured me that even though I was not Catholic he held me in the highest esteem and thought I was "worthy" of Jon. But he insisted I would have to change if I wanted the relationship to be long-term and serious. Jon, he frowned, shaking his head, could never commit to a woman who didn't believe in God. I should have been insulted, but I was amused and touched by Stephen's concern. In spite of his blunt assessment of me, his odd brand of respect shone through. His "spiritual direction" fell on mostly deaf ears, but I was making mental notes.

Jon and Stephen were also friends with Kim. Kim was tall, thin, and beautiful, with a sunny smile and an even sunnier disposition. Why did she have to be Catholic, too? I hated her for it. Kim was kind, virtuous, esteemed by Stephen as some sort of Madonna, and was a close friend of my Catholic boyfriend. Standing next to her I felt like a dirty sneaker kicked too close to a gleaming glass slipper. Sometimes at parties, Kim nursed one beer all night while brushing off the crude comments of flirtatious drunks with a blushing, "Oh, you guys, you don't *mean* that." I wanted to kill her. I made fun of her, but I also made a mental note: *There's a different way to live.*

Jon eventually transferred to another school, and we broke up; I knew we would never survive long-distance, but I filed Jon's goodness away in the Catholic registry I was subconsciously compiling. I'd certainly seen hypocrisy that landed in the debit column, but I credited Jon, Stephen, and Kim with showing me that serious, religious young adults who lived what they believed were not mythical creatures. Such a life was possible. *Not for me*, I thought, *but it's possible.*

Their Actions, Their Impact

Over the next few years, my drinking increased and depression worsened. I quit school, planning to move back home to get my life together, but my parents had just accepted jobs in another state. I didn't want to move, so I was on my own, and fumbled my way through the next few years. I took an entry-level job at a marketing company and worked my way up the corporate ladder. That led me to the next set of Catholics I would encounter, women who surprised me with unbidden acts of bravery.

My management position required occasional travel to trade shows. On one trip, my colleague Caroline and I didn't have a meeting until late Sunday morning. She rose early, showered, dressed in her crisp navy blue suit, and made a phone call. Through the haze of my hangover I asked what she was doing. "I'm going to Mass," she said simply, pulling back the curtain to keep an eye out for her cab. I had nothing to say as I burrowed back under the covers. I wanted to mock her but suddenly nothing about what she was doing seemed funny. She was in control; she stood for something. I felt a glimmer of respect.

Sometime after that, one of my employees, a single woman, became pregnant. Martha told me that she was Catholic. An abortion was not an option. She would have the baby and put it up for adoption. I was stunned. "An abortion would be so simple," I said. "Why let one mistake ruin your life?" I reminded her that both her mistake and her choice could remain private. That's what *Roe v. Wade* was all about. But she was steadfast. Her love for the child she carried reached a place deep inside me. I was shaken. What did I believe in that deeply?

By the time I was in my late twenties, I admitted to myself that I was a desperately unhappy woman. Years of drinking hadn't erased any of the pain I'd battled, and though I couldn't imagine continuing down the same road, I didn't know where else to turn. I had no belief system, nothing I could cling to in a crisis. I lacked a cohesive philosophy of life, but I realized one thing: I wanted a rock. I yearned for the strength and bravery I had seen in others.

When I pondered what it would be like to have a concrete set of beliefs instead of the fragile mosaic I'd created from the sand of secular culture, I considered the lives of people I'd known. How did other people live? What had I learned from that subconscious registry I'd compiled?

There was Jack, with his Catholic upbringing. He'd taken a dramatic detour from his faith in his twenties, but eventually returned to the Catholic Church. From the moment we became friends, Jack was there for me, no matter how removed I was from the faith and morality he embraced. I thought of Jack's mother, Loretta, her gathering-in of the lost, the family's acceptance of strange, heathen me. There was Jon, solid, unwavering. Stephen and Kim. I remembered Caroline, calling a cab from a hotel room as I slept off too many Bloody Marys. And Martha. Oh, the thought of Martha made my heart hurt. Having her baby no matter the cost in time, dollars, or peer ridicule. Martha touched me at a level so deep, I didn't know I could feel that way anymore.

Other pictures sprang to mind, too: the mockery of classmates when I realized I was "nothing." The manipulation of someone I'd trusted, attempts to trick me into salvation by pizza. Catholics who slept around on Friday nights and slipped into pews on Sunday morning, as if life was a box of tidy compartments that didn't touch one another.

In the trial for religion, I'd filed away all sorts of testimony. I'd known genuine practitioners and transparent posers. At various times, I'd been hurt, angered, repelled, indifferent, and attracted.

I knew now what I wanted.

I had been watching people, consciously or subconsciously, all my life. I had tallied points without knowing that's what I was doing. In the final analysis, the witness of people whose faith was honest, sturdy, and real swayed me. They had faith that they openly lived, faith real enough to change lives, as it was changing mine. These witnesses had faith that challenged and sometimes scared them, made them blush, put them in positions of ridicule. They stood tall and held fast, and their faith in God was so radiant it couldn't be dimmed, contained, or compartmentalized.

That was the faith that shone on me, made me squint and blink, and initially look away as it blinded me with its oddity, until one day when I realized something about these people. Theirs was a light I wanted to soak up. I wanted that kind of brilliant conviction to burn away my pain and transform my soul into something dazzling and new.

Until I saw how some people lived, I hadn't believed in God. But thanks to a faithful, resplendent cloud of witnesses who modeled real Christianity for me, a new light was dawning.

These people were the evidence that God believed in me.

CHAPTER 2

Do Fall in Love with Jesus

"You mean you literally put your *lips* on it and kissed it? A piece of wood?"

Jack nodded and munched on a French fry.

"This isn't some weird metaphor for what you were *thinking*," I asked, "or for what you *wanted* to do?"

He shook his head.

"You *actually* walked up to this cross and you *kissed* it?"

He nodded again. "Yup," he said. He ate another fry.

I took a sip of coffee and absorbed the story and the image. This was weird. Catholics were weird.

"*Why?*"

"Well," he said, "it's like this. On Good Friday, Catholics always do this. They have a service—I mean, *we* have this service. I guess I'm one of them again. It's not a Mass, 'cuz it's the only day of the year when we don't have Mass—but it's this service where we have veneration of the cross. Do you want me to explain veneration?"

"Please."

"Okay," he said. "Veneration means showing respect ... honor. We're honoring Jesus' sacrifice for us by showing honor to the cross, because it was on the cross that he died for us, right? So kissing the cross is kissing the symbol of his sacrifice."

"Do you *have* to kiss it? What if you feel weird about kissing a piece of wood?"

Jack smiled. "You don't *have* to kiss it. There are other ways to show respect. You can genuflect, or you can bow, or you can just touch it if you want to. But I wanted to kiss it. I couldn't *wait* to kiss the cross."

I shook my head, not fully able to grasp this idea. Kissing an inanimate object. In public. It was too far out of the realm of my experience; it smacked of "cult." Jack was going through a program at his church to learn, or relearn, about his faith as he made his way back to the Catholic Church he had left behind. Although I found most of what he told me incredibly odd, I was simultaneously intrigued.

In the glowing fluorescent light of a Perkins restaurant, Jack's story about feeling the power of God by kneeling down and placing his lips on a wooden cross unsettled me. This wasn't merely a pleasant little ceremony or a way to be politely respectful. He *felt* something. Deeply. Every time he talked about God these days— every time he talked about *Jesus*—it was like he was head over heels in love.

Better Than a Top Ten List

Whenever I see people immersed in things they're passionate about, I'm struck by the joy they radiate. Whether their passion is for art, sports, music, theater, hobbies, job, or family, it's irresistible and draws me in. Passion is magnetic. And when we encounter a soul who has genuinely fallen in love with Jesus, we encounter the most powerful kind of attraction. We don't even label what these people do as evangelization—they may not even be conscious of what they're doing. They're simply emanating love for God.

It makes sense. Compare deep, true love for Jesus with marriage: If we want the world to know how marvelous the sacrament of marriage is, we hope to show them happy Catholic marriages. If we want the world to know how great Jesus is, we want them to see our love for him. If we want to transmit the idea that faith is life-changing, the world needs to see Jesus changing our lives. That kind of passion and relationship with the Lord is a far better witness than a top ten list about "Why Faith is a Good Thing."

Feelings, of course, can't be dictated. "Fall in love with Jesus" is not a prescription that we can run out and fill. But we can open ourselves to him and his love for us. If we've never felt that way before, we can start in a simple place. Take a look at people who radiate love for God. What are they doing that we're not? What's different about their prayer lives, their reading habits, their relationships? What can we, using their habits and practices as a starting point, begin doing that will ignite the flame?

Smitten by His Love

Pope Francis has said: "When one finds themselves with Jesus, they live the wondrous awe of that encounter and feel the need to look for him in prayer, in the reading of the Gospels. They feel the need to adore him, to know him and feel the need to announce him."[4]

The Holy Father also reminds us that Jesus poured out everything for us, that true love is complete self-donation: "The cross of Christ invites us also to allow ourselves to be smitten by his love, teaching us always to look upon others with mercy and tenderness."[5]

There was a time in my life when I couldn't imagine such things. Falling in love with God and announcing him to everyone? Embracing the cross and allowing suffering to soften my heart? It was inscrutable to me, as impenetrable as Jack's kissing of the cross sounded before I was a believer. When I genuinely began searching for faith, however, it was people who fervently loved God who attracted me. I can only hope and pray to become like my role models, people who have discovered, as Pope Francis said, the need to adore and announce Jesus, and share the reality of his love.

Differently Happy

My friend Liz, who converted to Catholicism after years of knowing vibrant, joyful Catholics, told me one day that her friend Sister Marie Therese "loves Jesus so much that it just pops out when you're around her. It's the way she talks, the way she acts—it's who she is. I became an oblate of the Benedictines before I ever became a Catholic, due to her example."

Like Liz, long before I was a Catholic, I noticed that some people seemed to have deeper pockets of joy than others. They were not lecturers, scolders, sermonizers, or judges. They had something I couldn't put my finger on, something down to earth but otherworldly. They emanated a sweet fragrance that I eventually found myself wanting to breathe in.

"There is a woman in my Spirit of Motherhood group," my friend Renee told me, "and I just love her. She is very faithful and happy, and that shows itself in joy *every time I see her*. She makes everyone around her feel loved. It's something you cannot fake."

My friend Holly told me about a similar woman who had a profound effect on her. Holly was raised in the Presbyterian Church and didn't embrace Catholicism until several years after she married Jack. Sometime in the first few years of her marriage, Holly met Pat. "She was first a stranger, then became a friend, and now we call her our godmother," Holly said. "Pat spoke to the youth group we helped with, and she shared story after story about miraculous things God had done in her life. I was amazed at her faith through all of those stressful, scary situations." Pat's life was far from perfect, had, in fact, never been easy, but she possessed a light that shone brightly on my friend.

Jen, another friend, grew up with such light. "My mom's faith is very much her walk with her friend, Jesus. She speaks to him, and about him, in a very informal, personal way. She's spent a lot of time listening for God.... I've always been attracted to the way she leans on the Lord."

Another friend, Karl, who grew up in a non-Catholic home, said his parents always surrounded their family with passionate Christians. As an adult, Karl converted to Catholicism, but he's always been grateful for a childhood that was populated with genuine disciples of Jesus who had a powerful impact on his faith.

These were the kinds of people I found myself returning to again and again when the sand was shifting beneath my feet. I craved a taste of what was on their plate, because they seemed so differently happy. Their joy didn't originate in material goods, or careers, or in worldly possessions. What they possessed was something above and beyond. One day, I finally had to admit that I wanted it, too.

Stir Us Up

Years ago, after I was received into the Catholic Church, a friend babysat my daughters while I attended RCIA team meetings at my new parish. Melinda was a devout evangelical Christian. When the subject of religion had first come up between us, she'd fixed her eyes on me and pursed her lips when I mentioned my recent choice of Catholicism. It didn't take long though before we were exchanging tales of what Jesus Christ had done in our lives. One day, with a note of skepticism in her voice, she said, "I've never heard a Catholic talk about Jesus the way you do."

"Really?" I said, genuinely surprised. "Well, you just haven't met enough Catholics!" She looked doubtful, and I laughed. "No, really," I continued, "I know plenty of Catholics who talk about Jesus this way."

That was true. The new friends I had made in my parish, and our RCIA leader, were serious Christians who worshiped with eagerness and fervor and sought the Lord's will in their lives. On the other hand, I knew what Melinda meant. A "typical" evangelical Christian and a "typical" Catholic do not necessarily employ the same vocabulary when they speak about their Lord and Savior. But once we knew each other well enough to share details of our faith lives, we realized we were often saying the same things: *I love God ... I love my faith ... the Mighty One has done great things for me.*

I said those words so often to myself: *The Mighty One has done great things for me.* I remember driving to Mass one weekday evening when I was still a newish Catholic. The sun was just beginning to droop in the sky behind me as I drove into town. The fall weather was crisp and full of the promise of my favorite season. Everything felt peaceful and right and whole: my marriage was in the best shape it had ever been in, my two little girls were healthy and happy, and I loved being a mother. But there was another feeling, too, something that felt even bigger, overarching, and underlying everything I did. As I drew closer to the church, to my new parish—*my new home,* I thought—I was overcome with a feeling of anticipation, a quivering kind of bliss. I couldn't *wait* to get to the church, could hardly contain myself as I thought of the Eucharist. I couldn't wait to be with the Lord.

The ability to go to Mass whenever I wanted was an enormous privilege. I was going to be with Jesus again, to receive his Body and Blood, and spend time with him in prayer. I felt like a kid at Christmas. The words of St. Augustine were fitting and right:

Stir us up, and call us back; inflame us, and draw us to
Thee; stir us up, and grow sweet unto us; let us now love
Thee, let us run after Thee.[6]

My life seemed too good to be true. The ugliness and pain of
my past was erased every time I received Jesus. In the Holy Sacrifice of the Mass, in my encounters with him in the confessional,
or immersed in prayer at home, I was lavished with undeserved
gifts. Was this what Jack had felt when he was falling in love with
God?

Practicing What They Preach

Priests are only human. Like the rest of us they are imperfect, but
the priests I have known are overwhelmingly open, generous,
faithful men who love Jesus and fervently desire to serve God.
They express their love in a variety of ways, according to their gifts
and how the Lord wishes to use them, but some possess such a visible and profound love for the Lord that they are beacons to others.
    I had been Catholic for a couple of years when I met newly
ordained Fr. Joe. I was on the RCIA team, and he was our team director. I had an appointment with him one day to talk about some
RCIA business, but first I stopped in at the church to pray. I then
headed next door to the parish offices. Fr. Joe must have seen me
coming from the direction of the church, because he said, "Have
you been visiting him?"
    Visiting him? I'd never really heard it put that way. I was "pray-
ing before the Blessed Sacrament." I was "at adoration." I was ...
well, what was I? I was a Christian, for Pete's sake, and I was even a
Catholic now—why did Father's phrasing sound funny?
    It took me a moment, and then I realized what it was. Fr. Joe's
description of my time with Jesus didn't sound like most Cath-

olics' description of adoration. His way sounded so much more personal. That resonated and was what I loved about it. I *did* feel that personal connection, too, but I'd rarely heard a Catholic, apart from Jack, express it that way. Fr. Joe's easy manner gave me permission to talk about falling in love with Jesus. Such vocabulary was freeing. And it was just as Catholic, just as appropriate and accurate, I realized with relief, as more formal ways of expressing our love for him.

I remember many occasions, after that day in Fr. Joe's office, when I stopped in at the church to visit Jesus in the Blessed Sacrament. Fr. Joe was often there, too, spending time with his Beloved, living and practicing what he preached. Fr. Joe became my spiritual director, and to this day, when I see him for confession or to seek counsel, I am always struck by the quiet, holy, and tangible love for Jesus that flows out of him.

Fr. Joe's love for the Lord had a powerful effect on my friend Danae as well. In high school, Danae was attracted to a non-Catholic, evangelical brand of Christianity and fell away from her Catholic faith. Ironically, it was precisely Danae's deep love for Jesus that left her susceptible to wandering. Providentially, it was a Catholic, evangelical priest's deep love for Jesus that helped to bring her back. Danae said:

> I just felt like Catholicism was about rules and not about Jesus. I was attracted to my Protestant friends' intimacy with the Lord. I didn't see many Catholics who had that (I failed to notice that many of them did—I just wasn't looking in the right places). The Protestants seemed to have the lingo, and they knew their Bibles *so* well. I didn't know *any* Catholics who read the Bible (again, I failed to notice that we read from it every day at Mass, not to mention the Divine Office). I just wanted a church that emphasized a relationship with Jesus. And whenever I had questions

about the teachings of the Catholic Church, there were never answers that satisfied me.

Danae's faith in Christ was vibrant, but she couldn't see relevance in her Catholic upbringing. She continued:

Once I left home for college, I stopped attending Mass, except for occasionally playing piano for the student Mass. After my freshman year, I was home for the summer and my best friend and I wanted to start a youth group. My parents suggested we contact a new priest in our parish. I had no interest in a Catholic youth group, but for some reason I gave that priest a call. He was so excited about our idea because he'd been praying to the Holy Spirit to start a young adult group. I explained that we weren't keen on the Catholic faith. He said that was okay, he would just meet with us and talk. That began a summer of meetings where I encountered the Catholic faith in a way that I never had before. Fr. Joe talked in that "evangelical style" but also answered every single one of our questions with facts and information that could not be disputed.

Danae and her friend ran head-on into the reality that Catholicism is vibrant and alive. Fr. Joe offered comprehensive, intelligent responses to all of Danae's questions, demonstrating that faith and reason work seamlessly together in the Catholic Church. He made a tangible difference in Danae's life:

... he showed me what it meant to have a relationship with the Lord in the Catholic Church. It's hard to argue against the beauty and awesomeness of the truth that is found there. Hard to argue that you can best have a relationship with the Lord through the life-giving sacraments, especially the Eucharist. Basically, God used a holy priest (and other great witnesses) to open my eyes to what was always right in front of me. He helped my head and my heart understand that the Catholic Church is all about Jesus and that the greatest intimacy we can have is receiving his precious Body and Blood.

Danae would later make a similar difference in the faith of her future husband. She marks her friendship with Fr. Joe as a turning point.

Walking the Walk

Simply by living the faith that they love, holy priests attract our attention. As Pope Francis said:

> We know well that with Jesus life becomes richer, and that with him it is easier to find meaning in everything. This is why we evangelize. A true missionary, who never ceases to be a disciple, knows that Jesus walks with him, speaks to him, breathes with him, works with him. He senses Jesus alive with him in the midst of the missionary enterprise. Unless we see him present at the heart of our missionary commitment, our enthusiasm soon wanes and we are no longer sure of what it is that we are handing on; we lack vigor and passion. A person who is not convinced, enthusiastic, certain and in love, will convince nobody.[7]

Fr. Scott, another priest who became a friend, is a humble, holy man who is convinced, enthusiastic, certain, and in love. From the moment my family and I met him, we knew we were in the presence of someone who loves Jesus with his whole heart, mind, soul, and strength. That love is seen in the little things.

Over one of the first dinners at our house (and he became a regular guest), Fr. Scott and I talked about writing and blogging. Though he had once maintained a blog, by the time we met he had deleted his blog from cyberspace. It was clear he loved writing, so I was perplexed as to why he'd given up a harmless writing outlet.

But it wasn't always harmless, he countered. The blog world, even among religious, can degenerate into pettiness and competition. Who is funniest in the blogosphere? The smartest? Who's snarkier, the most clever? Who is quickest with wise and holy assessments of what's happening in the Catholic world?

Fr. Scott is the first to say that it's possible to blog without succumbing to such temptations, but he felt that when *he* wrote online about the issues he was passionate about, it was too easy to be personally tempted to descend into a lack of charity. So he decided to bow out. Though his blog had gathered a robust following, the popularity and kudos weren't worth the dangers to his soul. He hit the "Delete" button. Blog gone. Peace of mind returned. It was my first encounter with his witness of detachment.

Fr. Scott doesn't deliberately witness about simplicity and humility, but his life speaks volumes. He drives a simple car and prefers a simple home. At one point, he was even embarrassed by his kitchen. The hundred-year-old rectory in which he lived needed renovation. His parishioners knew Fr. Scott loved to cook. Donations were raised and the tiny, old kitchen was demolished and replaced with a shiny new one featuring state of the art appliances, marble countertops, and ample storage space. It was a chef's dream but Fr. Scott was a bit abashed, even though he knew it would benefit many priests who would come after him.

Although he loves to read and loves books—he once owned twenty-three copies of his favorite book, *Pride and Prejudice*—he no longer owns more possessions than he can pack into his car. His priority is his love for God and God's people and for spreading the Gospel of Jesus Christ. Living in a materially simple way helps him do that.

A Thing Like a Love Affair

To say, "Fall in love with Jesus!" as if it were just another piece of advice sounds facile. But the reality stands: Love *is* the most powerful witness. Of St. Francis of Assisi, G. K. Chesterton said, "To this great mystic his religion was not a thing like a theory but a thing like a love affair."[8]

A love affair with God may sound odd. I once saw an article in which the writer objected to "love affair language" because, he said, "Jesus is not my boyfriend!" And while it's true that we don't want to diminish the nature of our relationship with God in any way, there is nothing juvenile or belittling about the imagery of God as our Beloved. Such imagery is as old as the Song of Solomon. Both ancient Jewish and Christian traditions have likened the marriage relationship to our relationship with Our Lord. St. Bernard of Clairvaux said:

> To love so ardently then is to share the marriage bond; she cannot love so much and not be totally loved, and it is in the perfect union of two hearts that complete and total marriage consists. Or are we to doubt that the soul is loved by the Word first and with a greater love?[9]

There is nothing small or pedestrian about the breadth and depth of love God wants from us. It's true that this love affair doesn't mean we'll wander around in a giddy stupor. Just as in marriage, authentic love is more than the infatuation we feel when we first fall in love. Love is sustained and grows deeper through repeated acts of the will and through lifelong commitment. The same is true of our faith in and love for Jesus Christ.

We fall in love, commit, and promise to live that commitment for the rest of our lives. Love is the anchor—in both marriage and faith—that will hold us in place when dryness, boredom, suffering, and hard times set in. The initial consolations of both earthly and divine love steel us for the future. In both cases, we know that the puppy love phase will pass, but its consolations will ripen our souls for the richness to come.

At its core, our connection to Jesus Christ is a relationship of love. "We, the women and men of the Church," said Pope Francis, "we are in the middle of a love story: each of us is a link in this chain of love. And if we do not understand this, we have understood nothing of what the Church is."[10]

I don't know about you, but I know what I want: I want to be a link in that chain. I want to love Jesus with the urgency of one who can't wait to kiss the cross on Good Friday. I want to be like Renee's friend, who can't fake the joy that buoys her into every room. I want the passion for Christ that Karl grew up with and the irresistible faith of Sister Marie Therese. I want to talk to my friend Jesus every morning as Jen's mom does, and share stories like Pat's, stories of miracles that change lives. I want to hold fast to the witness of holy men like Fr. Scott and Fr. Joe. I want to recall, fan, and keep alive the flame that made me so eager to get to Mass that I couldn't drive fast enough.

What do I want? I want a thing like a love affair.

"When I am completely united to you, there will be no more sorrow or trials; entirely full of you, my life will be complete."

—St. Augustine[11]

CHAPTER 3

Do Hang Out with All Kinds of People

SOMETIMES I THINK IT'S A LITTLE TOO EASY for us Catholics to hang out with only our Catholic friends. It's natural to want to be bolstered by those who understand and share our values. I need such community as much as anyone, and there are huge benefits to finding and nurturing that kind of support, perhaps especially for converts such as Tom and me. It's crucial to cultivate a Catholic culture in our lives and, more expansively, in our world.

At the same time, since we are called to be in the world but not of it, sometimes we have to enlarge our sphere of contact and open ourselves to the surprises the Lord has in store for us. I'm reminded of a passage from J. D. Salinger's *Catcher in the Rye*:

> I knew this one Catholic boy, Louis Shaney, when I was at the Whooton School ... after a while, right in the middle of the ... conversation, he asked me, "Did you happen to notice where the Catholic church is in town, by any chance?" The thing was, you could tell by the way he asked me that he was trying to find out if I was a Catholic. He really was. Not that he was prejudiced or anything, but he just wanted to know. He was enjoying the conversation about tennis and all, but you could tell he would've enjoyed it more if I was a Catholic and all.

That kind of stuff drives me crazy. I'm not saying it ruined our conversation or anything—it didn't—but it sure as hell didn't do it any good. That's why I was glad those two nuns didn't ask me if I was a Catholic. It wouldn't have spoiled the conversation if they had, but it would've been different, probably. I'm not saying I blame Catholics. I don't. I'd be the same way, probably, if I was a Catholic.... All I'm saying is that it's no good for a nice conversation. That's all I'm saying.[12]

I live in a small town. Our Catholic home-schooling group is microscopic. If we socialized only with other Catholic home-schoolers, my family would miss out on some amazing people. This is the story of one of the families we met, of a friend who made me glad my first question wasn't, "Did you happen to notice where the Catholic church is in town, by any chance?"

Kindred Spirits

We are not a soccer family. My idea of a great sport is to see who gets to the couch first to grab a nap, but several years back we gave soccer a try at the local YMCA with my then eight-year-old. The weather that first morning was bracing, far chillier than I thought a Saturday in April ought to be. As I glanced around, shivering and mentally calculating how much of my daughter's game I'd miss if I drove home to bundle up my two-year old, I realized the real soccer moms had brought blankets. I must have looked forlorn, and I assuredly looked cold, because the diminutive woman with bobbed black hair and a perpetual smile (*Hey, isn't she the one I keep seeing at the library with two children in tow?*) appeared at my side, like a genie ready to grant my wish. She offered me a blanket as she glowed with good cheer.

"Isn't it *wonderful?*" she chirped. "I love a crisp morning!"

I am equal parts not a morning person and not a cold-weather person, so I was tempted to cock an eyebrow and snort that "crisp" didn't describe the numbness in my toes. However, though I'm not a morning/cold-weather person, I am a polite one. I wrapped the much-appreciated blanket around my shivering two-year-old and thanked this sweet woman for whom I was very grateful.

I introduced myself, or maybe she introduced herself. We started chatting. Our daughters, it turned out, were on the same team. Her daughter, Laura, and my daughter, Lizzy, had already hit it off. Rose was a stay-at-home mom. So was I. We grabbed coffee from the concession stand and talked nonstop. Rose was delightful, sweet, intelligent. I was lucky to have been in need of a morning person's extra blanket that day.

It wasn't until we had gotten together a couple more times that we discovered we were both home-schooling moms. I thought Rose would fit in perfectly with some of my other friends, especially the moms in my Catholic home-schooling group. Except Rose wasn't Catholic. No problem. I looked for activities that our children could do together.

What struck me about Rose was just how kind she was. She was also thoughtful, generous, respectful of everyone she met, and sensitive to the feelings of all those around her. She had a habit of referring to her favorite things as "Magical!" And when Rose said something was "*Magical!*" she had a way of making me believe it, too. Magic, in some form, always seemed perched on Rose's shoulder.

She was also an answer to prayers. As a home-schooling mom, I constantly assess how I'm doing: Am I meeting my children's needs? What do I need to change, add to, or delete from our curriculum? Just before I met Rose, I'd been feeling anxious that our curriculum was lacking in science experiments and art projects. I hadn't expressed any of this to her, but, out of the blue, Rose suggested that we sign the kids up at the arts center for the home-school classes they'd just begun offering. "*Their classes are magical!*" she said. (They were.) She then announced she'd been feeling the tug to teach a science class. I asked if she had some scary mind-reading ability because she had just addressed two of my most pressing home-schooling concerns.

Our kids dissected owl pellets, constructed papier-maché volcanoes, blew up film canisters with Alka-Seltzer, and did loads of other science-y things that I had a tendency to Google but not actually do. Rose had a long-lasting effect on me, too. By their high school years, I was letting my daughters dissect frogs at the kitchen table.

On top of the art and science classes, Rose started a girls' club. She led us in crafts, service projects, and a camping trip, something I would gladly have given an admiring nod to had I seen it in a brochure, but Rose actually made it happen.

When club meetings were over, or the kids had abandoned owl pellets and run off to play, Rose and I cleaned up, disinfected surfaces, and chatted over coffee. We shared stories of our pasts, and compared notes about how we'd become home-schoolers. When I first mentioned that I wrote articles for Catholic publications, she laughed.

"That is *weird!*" she said, eyeing me as if I'd somehow planned this. "My best friend in the last place we lived was Catholic, too. Isn't that *funny*? Why do I always end up with Catholic friends?"

"I don't know. Do you try to spot the Catholics in a crowd?"

She laughed again. "Not on purpose. But I guess you never know!"

Not Exactly Jesus

One day, Rose mentioned religion again. I asked if she and her husband went to a church.

"No," she explained. "He grew up with the Methodist church, but he's not really active in anything right now. And I don't think he'd consider even *talking* about a Catholic church," she said.

"Oh, I didn't mean—", I said, but she cut me off.

"I know you didn't! No, don't worry about that! It's fine. It's not that I'm looking, exactly. I just find it kind of interesting. Catholicism, I mean. But I don't really believe in it. I guess you could call me, if anything, a Unitarian. Is that the right word? If I don't believe in Jesus exactly?"

"Yes," I said, "that would be the word, if that's what you mean—that you have a belief in God but not in the Trinitarian God? Not the Father, Son, and Holy Spirit?"

"Yes," she said, "Unitarian, then. I guess if there were a Unitarian church here I might go."

Conversations like this came and went as naturally as the kids ran in and out of Rose's back door.

My work somehow came up again one day. Rose asked more specifically about what I wrote, so I told her about my blog, and she expressed interest in reading it. I reminded her that the blog had a definite Catholic bent. I didn't want her to think I was pushing anything on her. She said that was fine. She was just curious to read some of my writing, and we left it at that. If she had more questions, I knew she would ask them.

Rose and I were becoming close friends. We talked about everything: motherhood and family, home-schooling philosophies, our families of origin, moving and starting over, favorite foods, teaching math, and how to construct the best Harry Potter costume for Halloween. And as easily as we talked about everything else, we talked about faith.

Trusting that neither was trying to persuade or change the other, our conversations about religion were never tense or uncomfortable. I shared stories of my conversion, especially as they related to my marriage and the adjustments Tom and I had gone through. Rose asked interesting questions and was always honest about and respectful of our differences.

Rose had a degree in chemistry and was fascinated by all branches of science. I remember when she asked what I thought about Body Worlds. She was hoping to go to the international anatomy exhibit that uses real human bodies to display various organ functions, the effect of diseases, and so on. She wondered what Catholics thought of the exhibit, whether it did or didn't mesh with our faith, and what the Church taught about such things. She'd waited to mention it until my children were out of earshot, in case it was something that would disturb them or was in opposition to our faith. Her sensitivity to my daughters' feelings on what to her was a purely clinical subject touched me. That single question led to others and to more extensive discussions about Catholic positions on science, ethics, faith, and reason.

His Plans vs. Mine

A couple of years into our friendship, I sensed that Rose was opening the door to a closer examination of Catholicism. We'd had a conversation that was particularly intense, and she'd expressed longing for more in her life. Shortly after that, something came up with her husband's job, and, before I knew it, their family was moving to the West Coast. My kids and I were heartbroken to lose our friends.

On top of my personal feelings, I was annoyed with the Lord. "What are you *doing*?" I asked him. "She was showing genuine interest in the Church, and now you're going to let her move away?"

Rose did move, and we stayed in touch, but between her busy life and mine, we didn't talk as often as we wanted to. A couple of years after their move, our families got together for a short vacation. There had been no discernible movement on Rose's part toward the Church, but, strangely enough, she'd made another friend in her new town who was a devout Catholic. But Rose reemphasized something she'd said long ago: her husband would never convert to Catholicism.

One night Rose called me with devastating news. Her husband had moved out. I felt helpless, living hundreds of miles away. I knew of only one thing our whole family could definitely do. We prayed for as stable a home life as Rose and the kids could maintain under such difficult circumstances and that Rose could trust God—however she currently perceived him—to get her and her children through this ordeal.

About a year after Rose's husband left, our family was able to swing another trip to visit them. Rose told me story after miraculous story about how the daily needs of her children were being met, usually just as she couldn't foresee where the next bit of financial stability would come from. It was still a heartbreaking situation, but God seemed to be taking care of them.

For our part, our family just kept praying. Every night, we prayed for Rose and the kids. Every time we went to Mass, we prayed. Every morning before we started school, we prayed.

One day, months after our last visit, Rose called me.

"Are you sitting down?" she asked me. I got a knot in my stomach. What could have happened now? There was fear in my voice as I asked her what was going on.

"No, it's good news!" she said. "And a question."

I was intrigued. "O-o-o-kay," I said. "I'm sitting down now. What is it?"

"Laura and Mackenzie and I are going to be baptized at the Easter Vigil this year. We're going to join the Catholic Church."

"*What?!*" I'm certain I shrieked. "Rose! I can't believe it! What's been going on? Tell me everything!"

She shared the astounding ways God had been at work—her own conversion and that of her two daughters, who had experienced many of the same things Rose had been feeling, thinking, and coming to believe. All three of them would be baptized, confirmed, and received into the Church at Easter.

"Now for the question," Rose said. "I was wondering ... will you be Laura and Mackenzie's godmother? Or is that too much to ask? Is it too much to be godmother to two people at once? I have no idea how this stuff is supposed to work! If it's too much, just tell me."

Through tears and laughter, I told Rose no, it was not too much, it could *never* be too much. "But are you sure you want me?" I asked her. "I know how much your friend there has helped you, what a blessing she's been. It would not hurt my feelings in the least. You should choose whoever you really want to do it."

"We want you," she said simply. "I do, and the girls do. If you don't mind. You have been the one constant in all of this."

If I don't mind.

I cried (Again? More? I don't remember if the tears ever stopped through that conversation.) and Rose promised to get back to me with details. I got off the phone and shouted out to my family that Rose and the girls were coming home to the Catholic Church.

He Who Has Jesus

I felt so unworthy when Rose called me a constant in her life. We lived hundreds of miles apart, and through some of the darkest hours of her life there were so many things I couldn't do, help with, or change for her. I didn't feel constant and certainly didn't deserve any credit for her conversion to Catholicism. But to see it unfold, to be her companion in even a tiny way on the journey, was, and remains, a great privilege. The true constant in Rose's life was Jesus Christ. He had provided abundant evidence that he believed in her.

I never stopped praying that one day Rose would grasp that fact—that Jesus was right beside her, ready to carry her through every step of the rest of her life.

And when I saw my hopes and prayers become reality? It was, as I knew the moment would be, in Rose's word, "Magical!"

"We cultivate a very small field for Christ, but we love it, knowing that God does not require great achievements but a heart that holds back nothing for self. The truest crosses are those we do not choose ourselves.... He who has Jesus has everything."

—St. Rose Philippine Duchesne[13]

CHAPTER 4

Do Be Honest About Your Own Struggles

"THEY WANT YOU TO DO *WHAT*?" I asked my friend.

With an eye roll and a sheepish smile, Jack repeated himself, "It's called natural family planning."

"Jack," I said, shocked at his naiveté, "c'mon! I think that's called the rhythm method. And I think they also call it having lots of babies."

"I know," he smiled ruefully. "But they say it's not the same as it used to be. Supposedly, the woman can learn her fertility signs and then you work around those, and avoid having sex when you're fertile if you're trying to avoid a pregnancy."

I frowned: "*Avoid* having sex? When you're *married*? That would kind of ruin all the spontaneity, wouldn't it? And it doesn't sound very *natural* to me. It sounds clinical."

"Yeah," he said. "It's ... I don't know." He shook his head and shrugged, "I'm looking into it."

An Honest Ambassador

The personal stuff, the awkward stuff, the intimate stuff is hard to share. But, in the pursuit of faith and truth, it's the personal, awkward, intimate stuff that really helps. If my friend hadn't been willing to share what he waded through on the meandering path of his conversion, I'd have been at a loss when my own turn came.

Jack, as I've said, fell away from the Church as a young adult. But on second thought, perhaps "fell away" doesn't accurately describe Jack's case. When I think of fallen-away Catholics, I think of people who slipped quietly away, who didn't deliberately leave the Church but just sort of floated down a new or more convenient stream. That's sometimes the way. People drift imperceptibly, dropping a habit of prayer without thinking about it, or skipping Mass without meaning to. Then one day they realize they have no idea how they wandered so far from the home in which they were born.

Others, however, don't slip, float, or drift—they run. Jack had bolted in an effort to escape beliefs he couldn't live by anymore. He was on a mission to find out what life was really all about, and the Church as he knew it—the CCD he'd grown up with, the answers he'd gotten thus far—wasn't cutting it. He had also experienced clinical depression that led to genuine hopelessness and despair, and he was determined to understand the meaning of suffering.

Struggling to better know God, Jack began reading widely. He tried various approaches to spirituality and at one point immersed himself in Zen Buddhism. He traveled from Nebraska to California to spend a summer at the Tassajara Zen Mountain Center, hoping for an authentic and permanent transformation. When he got back, he sat zazen—seated meditation, the central practice of Zen Buddhism—and taught me how to sit zazen, too. I was always terrible about it though. No matter how hard I tried to be detached and meditative, I could never clear my mind enough to get anywhere near enlightenment. I was usually thinking about my aching leg muscles or where we were going to get a cup of coffee when we were done.

But now, after Zen, after nothingness, after abandoning beliefs in enlightenment and reincarnation and myriad other things that hadn't brought him any closer to happiness, Christianity was starting to make sense again. He was asking questions he'd never asked before, and finding answers that resonated in ways he'd never dreamed possible. As he located puzzle pieces and snapped them into place, a clear picture was forming. He was feeling drawn to Catholicism, as if it were a force field he couldn't resist. At the same time, though, the Church still confounded him.

As a young husband, Jack was specifically struggling with the Catholic Church's teachings on contraception. When he got married, Jack was not a practicing Catholic, and he and Holly had been married in Holly's Presbyterian church. Neither of them objected to artificial birth control, so it had never been an issue. Now, however, with a number of obstacles to rejoining the Church conquered, Jack had come face to face with the last and toughest issue. Jack and Holly had always been convinced that the Catholic Church simply didn't get it in the area of sexuality, but now they were doing some detective work.

Because he knew I was searching, too, Jack had sort of taken on the role of ambassador for the Church to me, sharing the exhilarating discoveries he was making, probably hoping that I would find them just as intriguing. In order to put a more attractive face on the institution he was coming to love, he could have hidden his own doubts and struggles, especially regarding intimate areas, but I'm so grateful he didn't.

His goal was always to find the truth. He told me of the joys and theological nose dives he experienced, no matter where they led him. This, then, was the model of evangelization that I learned: genuine, thoughtful searching and honest, open discussion.

What follows is the timeline of the struggle that Jack shared with me, the same struggle I would later wrestle with myself.

Obedience

Five years after he got married, in spite of the fact that he was still out of sync with the Church on contraception, Jack began taking holy Communion again. He had abstained from it for those five years because he didn't believe most of what the Church taught but now, for the first time in years, he was excited about his faith again. Jack wasn't entirely clear about Church teaching on the sacraments, but he thought their reception would enhance his growing relationship with Jesus. He asked a priest he'd known a long time, Fr. Nick, if he could meet with him for spiritual direction. Fr. Nick replied, "Well, it's not 'spiritual direction,' because you're not living as a Catholic, but I will meet with you."

At their first meeting, Jack protested to Father that he *was* Catholic. He explained that he'd been away from the Church but was eager to return. He had only the stickiest wickets left to deal with, and he thought receiving the Eucharist would help him do that. What did Fr. Nick think he should do?

Seeing that Jack didn't grasp the place of the sacraments in the process of returning to full communion with the Church, Fr. Nick suggested that Jack focus on one thing. "I think you should work on obedience," Father said.

"Obedience in what area?" Jack asked.

"Start with contraception," said Fr. Nick.

"Umm. No," Jack firmly replied.

"Then stop taking the sacraments," said Father, equally firm.

"But I've just started receiving them again!" Jack protested. "I finally feel like I'm reconnected. I think I'm receiving a lot of graces from the sacraments!"

Fr. Nick looked Jack squarely in the eye and said: "You'll receive *greater* graces if you abstain from the sacraments. You will receive *untold* graces from practicing obedience."

Jack was stunned. There was no way Holly would accept the drastic step of giving up birth control. Jack tried another tack: "By obedience, well, do you mean obedience in other stuff, too?"

"What kind of other stuff?" asked Father.

"What about stuff like driving the speed limit?" He was thinking about their upcoming trip to Chicago. Eight steady hours of obeying the speed limit sounded like an enormous stretch to an avowed lead foot.

"Yes, Jack," said Fr. Nick with a smile, "I would say that obeying traffic laws would count as an instance of obedience. If that's the one thing you want to start with, I think that would be a very good thing to do."

"Because this trip to Chicago—"

"Yes," Father nodded. "You don't have to convince me. Drive the speed limit, Jack. And stop taking the sacraments."

School of Obedience

"I'm a scofflaw," Jack said when he recently retold me this story. "If there's a rational reason to ignore a law, I'll do it. *Fifty-five miles an hour*. Do you know how slow that was?"

Not long after his meeting with Fr. Nick, Jack stumbled on a book called *School of Obedience* by Andrew Murray, a missionary born in the late nineteenth century. He read:

The way to be a blessing to the world is to be men of obedience; known by God and the world by this one mark: a will utterly given up to God's will.[14]

Utterly? What exactly was God's will regarding speed limits? Did he regard them as sternly as commandments? What about abstaining from the sacraments while using birth control? Was that God talking, or just an ornery priest? Did "utterly" *really* mean giving up birth control, opening up to the possibility of having children? Murray, Jack read, exhorted everyone to:

Give himself to Christ the Master, to be guided and used as he would have. And therefore I say to every reader who has taken the vow of full obedience—and dare we count

ourselves true Christians if we have not done so?—place
yourself at once and wholly at Christ's disposal.[15]

During what Jack later dubbed The Year of Obedience, he abstained from the sacraments and drove the speed limit, not only
on that trip to Chicago, but all the time. It remained the one thing
he did differently, and other than that he didn't actively work on
any other aspect of conversion. In unrelated ways, it was a difficult
year: Holly lost her job and her father died. It was hard to make
sense of things, Jack told me. How was God at work in this terrible,
painful year?

One afternoon, Jack and Holly lay down together in their bedroom to talk. When they had lain down, they seemed to be in precisely the same place they'd been before: they did not want to have
children, did not plan to give up birth control, and Holly did not
want to be Catholic. During the entire Year of Obedience, Jack had
not spoken to Holly about becoming a Catholic. But somehow, after that talk, by the time they arose from that bed and walked to
the kitchen, their plans included throwing out the pills, being open
to starting a family, learning about natural family planning, and
scheduling Holly's attendance at the Rite of Christian Initiation of
Adults classes.

Obedience Redux

Fast-forward several years. Jack and Holly are now Catholic, in
full communion with the Church, and they are the parents of two
young children. I, too, had come a long way, to say the least.

I'd been attending RCIA since the previous autumn. Lent was
approaching and I was wrestling with a decision. I'd already tack-
led numerous doctrines and had found answers for them all: the
male-only priesthood, purgatory, closed Communion, Marian
doctrines, confession, the pope, infallibility. Jack's honesty and

input about his own struggles had been invaluable to me as we'd spent countless hours over coffee discussing Catholic dogma.

But I had one more enormous obstacle: I did not want to give up birth control. I didn't agree with the Church on the subject, but I didn't want to be a Catholic unless I could honestly say I would be faithful to all the Church's teachings. I was facing the core issue of Catholicism: the Church's teaching authority. I had to answer a question I'd repeatedly posed to myself. Did I believe the Catholic Church had infallible authority in matters of faith and morals?

I had to admit it: I did. I now believed that the Holy Spirit actively guarded his Church. I'd been reluctant to face the implications of that admission, but the implication, regarding this issue, was clear. Accepting the Church's authority meant submitting to a teaching I didn't like.

I thought about the Gospel of Mark that says, "Whoever does not receive the kingdom of God like a child shall not enter it" (10:15). I pictured a small child, whining, "But why, Daddy? Why do I have to do that?" I knew from my own experience as a parent that sometimes the loving answer is, "Because I said so."

With first a sinking but then a soaring heart, I realized that the Lord was gently replying, in answer to my whiny protests: "Because I said so. I'm your Father." He was asking me, as a loving father sometimes does, to accept with trust what I did not yet understand.

I felt weak and simultaneously buoyed up. I knew I still had much prayer and study ahead of me, but I was about to enter my own time of obedience as I realized that trusting God sometimes means walking in the dark awhile.

What about my husband's reaction? Tom still rejected Catholicism but out of love for me he agreed to give up birth control and try natural family planning. He didn't understand it any better than I did, but said he would never force something on me that I found morally objectionable, especially when his preference was, as he put it, motivated solely by selfish interest.

Grace flowed. I didn't think of it at the time, but the truth of Fr. Nick's words to Jack rang out: *You will receive untold graces from practicing obedience.* After submitting to this teaching, I embraced the doctrines on marriage, sex, and contraception, and grew in knowledge about those perhaps more quickly than I had with anything else.

The Easter Vigil was approaching and one day I said to Jack, "If I join the Church at Easter ..."

"What do you mean 'if'?" he said. "I thought you were ready."

"Well," I said, "I still don't know *everything* there is to know about the Catholic Church."

"No one knows everything," he gently reminded me. "If you're waiting until you're the perfect Catholic, it will never happen."

Big Medicine

That spring, as I prepared to be received into the Church, I pondered what my first holy Communion would be like. I was overwhelmed, overjoyed, and humbled. "My soul magnifies the Lord," I often murmured, recalling the Magnificat of Mary in the Gospel of Luke. "My spirit rejoices in God my Savior ... he who is mighty has done great things for me, and holy is his name" (1:46-49).

My dear friend's struggles—both when he left the Church and when he returned—seemed initially to be only about him, about his personal objections and trials. But through my own conversion I've come to see that each of us is a part of the Body of Christ. We are links, as Pope Francis has said, in the chain of God's love. Jack's ongoing, sometimes brutal, honesty was often the push I needed to keep going, and keep searching. I saw God work miracles in Jack's life, and they fueled my hope that maybe, just maybe, he would work miracles in mine, too.

Honest struggles over doctrine and obedience culminated in the unforgettable Holy Saturday night when I received my first

Eucharist at the Easter Vigil, knowing that he who is mighty had done great things for me.

> "Here [in the Eucharist] a hand from the hidden country touches not only my soul but my body. Here the prig, the don, the modern in me have no privilege over the savage or the child. Here is big medicine and strong magic.... The command, after all, was Take, eat, not Take, understand."
> — C. S. Lewis, *Letters to Malcolm*[16]

CHAPTER 5

Do Engage the Culture

I WAS A TWENTYSOMETHING ATHEIST when Jack recommended a children's book to me. I hadn't read *The Chronicles of Narnia* as a child, so C. S. Lewis's *The Lion, the Witch and the Wardrobe* was unfamiliar. I settled in on the mattress on the floor of my sparsely furnished bedroom and began reading. The majestic, electric Aslan leapt off the page and captivated me. I fell swiftly and irreversibly in love. It was perhaps my first inkling of falling in love with Jesus, though I didn't know that yet. I knew one thing, though—I wanted to grab that great, mighty lion and hold on. Like Lucy and Susan Pevensie, I wanted to bury my face in his mane, inhale his sweetness, and never let go.

A number of years later, Jack gave me another children's book. Barbara Robinson's *The Best Christmas Pageant Ever* is a mirthful but moving story in which "awful old" Imogene Herdman and her siblings, a raggedy bunch from the wrong side of the tracks, wreak havoc on an annual Christmas pageant. The Herdmans show up at Sunday school one week because they've heard there are snacks, and where donuts lead, Herdmans follow. They crash in on the day the pageant is to be cast, worm their way into the proceedings, and Imogene snags the role of Mary.

Scripture is untrodden territory for the Herdmans. As rehearsals proceed, they express constant astonishment at the peculiar details of Jesus's birth. Finally, on Christmas Eve, Imogene, her freshly startled heart swelling with the terrible, beautiful reality of the holy infant, is walloped by the power of Jesus for the first time in her short, rough life. She can barely stand the weight of his glory:

> In the candlelight her face was all shiny with tears and she didn't even bother to wipe them away. She just sat there— awful old Imogene—in her crookedy veil, crying and crying and crying.[17]

And I could barely stand the glory of this image. I started sobbing, too. I loved scrappy little, awful old Imogene. Then I realized something. I loved her mightily because I *was* Imogene: the bereft little girl who'd never known Jesus but who one day collided headlong with the reality and dazzling power of him. The God of the universe bowled Imogene Herdman over, and she would never be the same. Neither would I.

The Christ Child reduced a hardened Herdman to tears, made the altogether sensible little Pevensie girls follow a mystical lion for the rest of their lives, and he crumbled my unbelief. Such is the power of Jesus, and of the stories written about him.

I wasn't raised on beautiful tales of Our Lord, but I know them when I encounter them. I know the enduring, compelling power of all kinds of stories. From Scripture and the lives of saints, sinners, and disciples, to Imogene, Aslan, and countless less explicitly religious tales that nevertheless chronicle sin, repentance, love, and redemption, to purely secular works in search of truth, art speaks powerfully to us. Art connects us to one another and to God.

Inklings

"There are only two or three human stories," said novelist Willa Cather, "and they go on repeating themselves as fiercely as if they had never happened before."[18]

Human beings have always created art as a way of questioning, dissecting, and celebrating the human experience. "Every genuine art form," said St. John Paul II in his *Letter to Artists*, "in its own way is a path to the inmost reality of man and of the world."[19] We share our stories in order to share our search for truth. Sometimes those stories have an overt connection to faith and at other times offer only an obscure inkling.

The faith connection is usually explicit in a hefty tome that tells the story of a saint, but a child who stumbles on her mother's book-club selection might not know what she's getting herself into. When she was nine years old, my friend Liz, who was not being raised Catholic and knew nothing of canonized saints, picked up her mother's current read and began flicking through it. At six hundred pages, it was more daunting than the usual suspects on a preteen's summer reading list, but something about the book beckoned to Liz more insistently than the next volume of Nancy Drew. Curious, she turned to the beginning and started to read:

> Soubirous knows that it is six even though the chimes of the parish church of St. Pierre had not yet rung for early Mass. The poor have the time in their bones. Without dial or bell, they know what hour has struck, for the poor are always afraid of being late.[20]

It was an unlikely source of captivation for a young girl, but Liz was hooked. She would reread *The Song of Bernadette* by Franz Werfel every year until she was twelve. After hitting her teens, she put it down and forgot about it for a long time, but for four years of her childhood, she annually declared it to be her favorite book in the world. When, almost sixty years later, after becoming a Catholic, she reread *The Song of Bernadette*, Liz couldn't believe she'd been so attached to it as a child. All she knew was that it had somehow transported her.

It's not surprising that Werfel's astounding work about a mystical adventure would capture the heart of a sensitive girl, but sometimes connections to faith are more tenuous. Secular works that at first glance seem far removed from God might seem dubious reading or viewing choices for those who are striving to live their faith. But every artistic endeavor must be judged on its own merits. Works that superficially seem antithetical to faith but are fundamentally about the search for beauty can convey powerful messages. The God-given impulse and desire to create beauty is an integral part of humanity's spiritual search. As St. John Paul II said:

> ... true art has a close affinity with the world of faith, so that, even in situations where culture and the Church are far apart, art remains a kind of bridge to religious experience. In so far as it seeks the beautiful, fruit of an imagination which rises above the everyday, art is by its nature a kind of appeal to the mystery. Even when they explore the darkest depths of the soul or the most unsettling aspects of evil, artists give voice in a way to the universal desire for redemption.[21]

Artists of all kinds seek meaning and search for answers—seek God, really—in ways that can look nothing at all like Christian faith. And yet, by virtue of their desire to plumb the depths of the human condition, they take tentative steps on that bridge to religious experience. Seekers are everywhere. They are writing books, reading them, discussing them, making movies, composing music, and painting. How do we meet on that bridge?

A Surprising Voice

When I first became a Christian and abandoned my old pro-choice views, Tom and I initially engaged in screaming matches over my newly adopted opinions. When I finally realized my screaming was fruitless (imagine that!), I switched to quiet discussion and witnessing. I prayed that the Lord would lead Tom to the truth in another way. I wasn't surprised that, in having our own children, his heart softened. But I was surprised by his reaction to a rereading of the classic novel *Brave New World*.

Aldous Huxley published his dystopian story in 1932. In *Brave New World*, human individuality has been systematically erased through genetic programming and dispassionate conditioning. A diverse society has been replaced with a carefully designed caste system. Sex has been completely disconnected from reproduction and is just one more sensory pleasure, alongside the use of a mood-altering drug, Soma, used to keep the masses pliable, satisfied, and sedate. Human beings, sorted according to their use and value to society, are created in bottles and grown in factory labs.

When Tom reread *Brave New World* for the first time since becoming the father of two beloved little girls, he was stunned by his reaction. He was stopped cold at a passage he'd read many times but that had never affected him so chillingly. He read the description of babies, mass-produced in bottles, and reduced to nothing more than utilitarian objects:

The hum and rattle of machinery faintly stirred the air.

"Give them a few figures, Mr. Foster," said the Director, who was tired of talking.

Mr. Foster was only too happy to give them a few figures.

Two hundred and twenty metres long, two hundred wide, ten high. He pointed upwards. Like chickens drinking, the students lifted their eyes towards the distant ceiling.

Three tiers of racks: ground floor level, first gallery, second gallery.

The spidery steel-work of gallery above gallery faded away in all directions into the dark.

Near them three red ghosts were busily unloading demijohns from a moving staircase.

The escalator from the Social Predestination Room.

Each bottle could be placed on one of fifteen racks, each rack, though you couldn't see it, was a conveyor traveling at the rate of thirty-three and a third centimetres an hour. Two hundred and sixty-seven days at eight metres a day. Two thousand one hundred and thirty-six metres in all. One circuit of the cellar at ground level, one on the first gallery, half on the second, and on the two hundred and sixty-seventh morning, daylight in the Decanting Room. Independent existence—so called.

"But in the interval," Mr. Foster concluded, "we've managed to do a lot to them. Oh, a very great deal."

His laugh was knowing and triumphant.[22]

Tom felt a creeping sense of horror as he saw the brave new world of reproductive freedom very differently than he ever had before.

To Read or Not to Read

Every few years, it seems that a new set of controversial young adult books explode on the scene and parents are saddled with decisions. Do we allow our children to engage with the latest arrival in the world of popular culture?

Personal reading preferences aside, fluency in the language of pop culture can be of great value. It's worth the time it takes to investigate what family, friends, neighbors, and children are reading, listening to, watching, and discussing. Sometimes that investigation goes beyond the detective work of parenting and the protection of our children to bring something rich and worthwhile into our lives, too.

The Boy Who Lived

The first book in the Harry Potter series was published when my daughters were young. I'd heard pros and cons from all corners, but I was so busy with home-schooling my little girls and reading loads of other great books with them that I did what any sensible, tired mommy would do: I simply ignored the whole phenomenon.

Ignorance is bliss for only so long, though. Eventually, I saw that Harry was a force I'd be forced to reckon with one way or another. The series had been around for several years when I decided that the only way to make an informed decision was to read it for myself. I checked *Harry Potter and the Sorcerer's Stone* out of the library and zipped through it. It was absolutely charming. I was surprised by the overarching themes: sacrificial love, friendship, the importance of free will, and doing what is right over what is easy. Harry had won me over.

I shared the book with my daughters as a read-aloud, and that led to a shared reading experience of the entire series as it unfolded. From the outset, I talked with my daughters about everything. We discussed Harry and his friends' strengths and weaknesses, their mistakes, their courageous choices. We talked about the ways in which the characters matured and how they stayed the same. We dug into Christian symbolism and the theme of free will.

Harry had us talking about sin, redemption, and dying for someone you love. We examined the books in light of Catholic teaching,
and I taught my children how to identify the difference between
occultism and the practice of magic—I used the *Catechism of the
Catholic Church* as my guide—and the definitions of such things
in fantasy literature. Later books sparked discussions of just war,
what actions are morally acceptable in war, euthanasia, and the
definition of mortal sin.

Reading the Harry Potter series with my daughters left us with
cherished family memories, but the experience was more than
that. It became a part of my daughters' education in critical thinking and discernment.

As Catholics living in a secularized society, educating our children for such critical reading is vital. Our children will encounter
countless, competing worldviews over the course of their lives.
I can either shield them entirely from the world, or I can practice what my friend, Alicia, a fellow home-schooling mom, dubs,
"controlled exposure." That characterization, which I first heard
when my children were very young, neatly summed up my own
instincts as a mother. "Controlled exposure" is just a fancy way of
saying that I investigate the flood of information that comes our
way and help my children navigate new challenges as they arise,
giving them more control and more exposure as they mature. We
carry on frequent, lively discussions, and along the way, my children learn how to discern whether and how something fits into
our Catholic faith.

Proceed with Caution

Another book series that initially sounded impossibly problematic
was Suzanne Collins's *The Hunger Games* trilogy. At first glance,
the premise was so disturbing that I was convinced we would give

the series a pass. Little did I know that Collins's stories are fine literature with a powerful message.

The three books in the series, *The Hunger Games*, *Catching Fire*, and *Mockingjay*, present us with a dystopian society and a government that controls citizens by means of an annual fight to the death among child combatants chosen in a lottery system. As I did with the Harry Potter series, I ignored the hype for a while. But one day I decided to read *The Hunger Games* for myself. I was blown away.

In the end, I loved the trilogy, but this was no toss-away adventure series. The books begged for discussion with my daughters, but isn't that precisely what literature does? And as parents and as the primary educators of our children, it's our job to teach, direct, and discuss. My older girls and I had in-depth talks about the story, approaching the subject matter seriously and with care.

I still remember my then-fourteen-year-old daughter waking me up one August night. It was about two o'clock in the morning, and I heard a whisper at my bedside, "Mom, I just finished *Mockingjay*. Can we talk?" We sat in the cool, dark living room, a late summer breeze blowing in through the window as we discussed the series' critique of politics and modern culture. We talked about war, the corrupting influence of power, selling one's soul for material or political gain. We talked about media manipulation, propaganda, the ethics of reality TV. We ruminated on questions about personal choices, about knowing who we are and what we stand for, about desperately trying to hold on to morality and truth in hellish circumstances.

In *The Hunger Games* series, just as I had with the Harry Potter series, I discovered a complex and layered vision of humanity. I was grateful to delve into compelling literature with my kids, and reading these books and many other series with my daughters was a gift. Our discussions afforded my girls opportunities to exercise and strengthen critical-thinking skills, discernment, and the sharpening of their Catholic vision.

Mad, Bad Men

As much as I enjoy sharing books and movies with my daughters, my husband and I have watched a few shows that our kids were not in on. Several years ago, Tom and I started watching two compelling TV shows: *Breaking Bad* and *Mad Men,* each of which became a cultural phenomenon. While they're not for children—and, in the case of *Breaking Bad*, not for the faint of heart—they are serious programs that tackle central issues about the human condition. They are also, I would argue, meticulously made art.

Breaking Bad is about an insecure high school chemistry teacher named Walter White who discovers he has lung cancer. Fearful for his family, he enlists the help of a former student to help him provide for their financial future. "Mr. White" learns how to cook methamphetamine in order to earn enough money to pay his medical bills and provide for his wife and children after he's gone. *Breaking Bad* ran for five seasons and brilliantly explored issues surrounding family, free will, ego, and the moral consequences of each and every one of our choices.

Mad Men, ostensibly about Madison Avenue adman Don Draper behaving badly in the 1960s, was at its heart about identity, the search for truth and happiness, acceptance of our brokenness, and, like *Breaking Bad*, the cumulative effect of our choices. It was, like *Breaking Bad*, a masterful creation that weekly had everyone talking.

Some assert that viewing TV shows or movies that depict any sort of immoral behavior can never be condoned for a Christian, or that such programs should not even be considered art. But many such depictions, as old as the Bible and as timeless as the story of David and Bathsheba, are stories of repentance and redemption. Don Draper's story is familiar to us, and we identify with it on some level, because his story is one of those two or three stories that keep repeating themselves with such ferocity.

While I agree it's imprudent to expose oneself to an occasion of sin, I also agree with the following quote attributed to Aristotle: "It is the mark of an educated mind to be able to entertain a thought without accepting it." One could expand on that and say it is the mark of a well-formed conscience, a well-catechized mind, and a firm faith, to be able to encounter art and be moved, rather than unmoored, by it. That said, we all have varying levels of sensitivity and thresholds of temptation, and it's up to each of us to discern for ourselves whether certain on-screen depictions cross a line. And there's always the fast-forward button, which we have made use of at times at our house.

Grab the Popcorn

A well-made movie is an artistic joy to behold, and for an excellent list of movies worth viewing, check out *The Arts & Faith 100* (http://artsandfaith.com/t100/). From 1928's *The Passion of Joan of Arc*, to *Babette's Feast* in 1988, to the 2001 Japanese animated film, *Spirited Away*, mainstream filmmakers have proven that theirs is a medium capable of bringing forth arresting beauty, which can serve as a bridge to religious experience.

On the lighter side of film, be sure to also check out *The Arts & Faith Top 25 Divine Comedies* (http://artsandfaith.com/t100/25_comedy.html). The top spot naturally goes to the enchanting movie *Groundhog Day*, in which shallow, cynical Phil Connors becomes inexplicably stuck in Punxsutawney, Pennsylvania, reliving the same day, Groundhog Day. Also included on the list are other bits of genius such as *The Princess Bride* and several of the Pixar masterpieces. (The list is too old to include 2015's *Inside Out*, a beautiful, touching, and insightful film about emotions and family relationships.)

Whether through the Pevensie children and Imogene Herdman, or in the stories of David and Bathsheba, Don Draper, Walter White, and Phil Connors, we encounter players in the human drama, people just like us. When their stories begin, they don't know that true happiness can be found only in God. But that is what stories—in both Scripture and great art—can do. They point us, explicitly or implicitly, to the only Source that can really provide us with everything that we need.

Culture of Encounter

However we choose to do it, engaging rather than shunning the culture can have profound, and profoundly happy, consequences. When we engage with friends, family, coworkers, and acquaintances about these stories—our stories—we can help spread the Good News. Checking in with friends in the morning to exchange takes on last night's episode, listening to the latest Imagine Dragons song and discussing indie rock with your atheist friend, curling up with your kids and a good book for a meaty discussion over hot chocolate are forms of evangelization. Charles Dickens, who told a few timeless stories himself, said:

> Everything that happens ... shows beyond mistake that you can't shut out the world; that you are in it, to be of it; that you get into a false position the moment you try to sever yourself from it; and that you must mingle with it, and make the best of it, and make the best of yourself into the bargain.[23]

Pope Francis knows. He challenged us to be firmly, solidly our Catholic selves and also fearless about diving into the world when he exhorted us to create a "culture of encounter" that can bring us together.[24]

Encounter the culture. It's waiting for good news.

CHAPTER 6

Do Remember That Conversion Comes in Stages

"I fled Him, down the nights and down the days;
I fled Him, down the arches of the years;
I fled Him, down the labyrinthine ways
Of my own mind...."

—*The Hound of Heaven*[25]

IF YOU TRIED TO PLOT A COURSE for the map of my conversion, it would look something like this: Start down the atheist highway, then veer into skepticism. Loop around to reincarnation, round back, head over to the shore of serious questions. Stop to take a look at Eastern religion and, finally, home in on theism. Keep moving onward to Christianity, then drive straight into Christian baptism, and—final destination—the Catholic Church.

Tom's map looks a little different. The starting point on his was baptism in the Lutheran church at a month old. By the time he was thirteen, he didn't care about religion, was agnostic for most of his adult life, then entered the Catholic Church in his early forties.

Jack has a different map. He was raised Catholic, questioned everything, turned it inside out, and chose to go back to the Catholic Church with a richer, fuller version of his faith. Other friends of mine were raised in non-Catholic traditions, encountered Catholics who made the Church seem magnetic, and then couldn't wait to be part of it. On the other hand, I know another man who waited twenty-five years for his wife to embrace Catholicism. So many road maps.

When wives worry that their husbands will never convert, parents fret about their children, or friends worry about friends, I want to wave a file full of success stories, my stack of miracles: Tom and me, Jack and Holly, and countless other conversions. Realistically, I don't have the authority to wave that file as a guarantee of anything. I have no prescience about how anyone's life will turn out and my anecdotal evidence is just that. My friend Meg is a good example. Meg's been hoping for nearly twenty years that her husband, who has always been a faithful Christian, will be received into the Catholic Church, but he's still not showing any signs. She says:

> Eighteen years later, and I'm still waiting. He's read the entire Catechism (something very few Catholics have done!). He comes to Mass with us at Christmas and Easter (but never in-between). We now have Catholic grandchildren (and he's gone to their baptisms). I still don't know what exactly is holding him back. He's even stopped going to the church he grew up in.... I get the sense that he's sort of in no man's land right now. He can't, for whatever reason, become Catholic, but he also can't really be part of the church he grew up in.

Should Meg give up?

But what would giving up entail? Would Meg stop going to Mass, cut out confession, stop praying? Of course not. Even when there's no outward evidence that conversion is imminent, we shouldn't give up. That doesn't mean we should pepper every interaction with annoying questions about why the other party won't convert, but it does mean that we can keep hope alive in our hearts.

In *Deathbed Conversions: Finding Faith at the Finish Line*, I wrote about thirteen people who either literally were received into the Church on their deathbeds or underwent conversions very late in life. Each one of them had someone in his or her life who never gave up: Oscar Wilde relied on his friend Robbie Ross, a fellow convert. John Wayne's first wife and his children prayed for years, and his friend movie director John Ford was a powerful witness who died with a rosary in his hand. Gary Cooper's wife and daughter never gave up either, even when he strayed from the marriage and caused his family great emotional pain.

History offers even more encouragement. St. Monica never gave up on her husband, Patricius, who was finally baptized shortly before he died. It was many more years before her wayward son, Augustine, saw the light. Monica even prayed for and saw the conversion of her mother-in-law.

Servant of God Elisabeth Leseur was already married when she experienced a conversion, but her husband, Felix, an atheist, wanted nothing to do with religion. Elisabeth died from cancer when she was just forty-eight and left behind a diary, which her husband read. He was so affected by his wife's witness of persistent prayer and hidden sacrifice that he converted and became a priest.

It's easy to despair, though, when we look at the big picture and see only that the world is a mess. There's so much over which we have no control. But St. Monica's fourth-century world was a mess, too, as was Elisabeth Leseur's at the end of the nineteenth century. We simply never know for certain what is unfolding interiorly in anyone, and even when hope seems lost, the Holy Spirit is at work, sometimes in stealthy ways. Set aside the gloominess of the big picture for a moment and zoom in on the detailed map of one soul. Is there one person God is calling you to pray for?

I used to get annoyed with the "Hound of Heaven" and the way he would infiltrate even my dreams. I once wrote in my journal:

I had a dream where I was in a crowded waiting room. Jack came in and said, "Jesus wants to see one of you."

"Oh, no!" I said. "I think it's me!"

The Lord is dogged in his pursuit.

It Takes a Long Time

"Beginnings are always messy," said British novelist John Galsworthy. Sometimes, in our eagerness to gather others into this fold that we love so much, we make other people's beginnings messier than they need to be.

I used to shout my new views at my husband. It didn't help. Holly told me that before she decided to join the Church, whenever Catholics smugly assumed she would convert, she felt a stubborn defiance rising in her. When an acquaintance at a youth group she helped with found out Holly wasn't Catholic, he said, "Oh, you will be, just wait!" She was indignant. "It felt like he wasn't treating me as an individual who could make up her own mind," she said.

Later, when she did enter RCIA as a tentative inquirer, still not certain she'd go through with anything, one of the first things her RCIA leader did was instruct them to pick a saint name for their group. "It seemed like they were pushing this difference in our faces. I *really* was not there yet," she said.

The beginning of conversion is rarely a Damascus-road affair that happens in one neatly defined moment or plays out in a predictable way. There are no guarantees about if or when conversion will happen. Fortunately, we don't have to worry about that, because we aren't the ones in charge. We do have control over some things: we can tend to our own ongoing conversion by way of prayer and the sacraments, and strive to live our faith with commitment and devotion. We can also be patient with those who are in various stages of conversion. "Have no anxiety about anything," the Letter to the Philippians tells us, "but in everything by prayer and supplication with thanksgiving let your requests be made known to God" (4:6).

Of the stages of conversion, George MacDonald, a nineteenth-century Scottish writer, poet, and clergyman, said, "As the world must be redeemed in a few men to begin with, so the soul is redeemed in a few of its thoughts and wants and ways, to begin with: it takes a long time to finish the new creation of this redemption."[26]

MacDonald could have been speaking of C. S. Lewis who, though they never met, later called MacDonald his spiritual master (MacDonald died in 1905, when Lewis was just seven years old). When Lewis was a young man and still an atheist, he read MacDonald's novel *Phantastes*. "That night," he said, "my imagination was, in a certain sense, baptized; the rest of me, not unnaturally, took longer.... I had not the faintest notion what I had let myself in for by buying *Phantastes*."[27]

The *Catechism of the Catholic Church* tells us:

> From the time of the apostles, becoming a Christian has been accomplished by a journey and initiation in several stages. This journey can be covered rapidly or slowly, but certain essential elements will always have to be present: proclamation of the Word, acceptance of the Gospel entailing conversion, profession of faith, Baptism itself, the outpouring of the Holy Spirit, and admission to Eucharistic communion. (1229)

While the Catechism here refers to the formal steps of Christian initiation into the Church, it is also helpful to take a closer look at the elements mentioned. "Proclamation of the Word" and "acceptance of the Gospel entailing conversion" are both steps that can take years and even decades. How long did it take Lewis to fully embrace the Word that first whispered to his soul in *Phantastes*? How long before St. Augustine accepted the Gospel? We have to allow time for the stages of conversion to take root.

"Who Are You?"

I spoke of my friend Jen in an earlier chapter—she was attracted to her devout Catholic mother's love for Jesus and deep prayer life. "She sat many mornings at our kitchen table with her journal, an open Bible, and a burning candle. She still does that," Jen said. Her mom likely presumed her daughter would never leave the Church, but by the time Jen was in college, she was not following in her mother's footsteps.

Like many young adults who move away for school, Jen drifted from the faith of her childhood. But her upbringing was not so easily shaken off. Though she was shedding old beliefs and embracing secular attitudes, she also remembers realizing that her Catholic identity had left an indelible mark. During a "Who Are You?" diversity exercise in one of her classes, while many students focused on racial or ethnic backgrounds to symbolize their culture, Jen found herself drawing a picture of a rosary.

After graduating from college, Jen's personal and professional network placed her squarely in the midst of communities that espoused moral relativism. She found herself enthusiastically adopting ideologies inconsistent with the Catholic faith. Her break from the Church was almost complete, but there was one tenet of the faith that she never left behind. She was still opposed to abortion. None of her pro-choice friends had been able to sway Jen on that particular (and to her friends, highly peculiar) position.

"No matter what someone explained to me about women's rights and privacy, they couldn't ever answer my questions about when life begins, at least not in an intellectually satisfying way," she told me. "If they argued it began at birth, then I wanted to know what the baby was before birth if it wasn't alive. If they argued it began earlier, I wanted to know why the mother's life and choices were more valuable than the child's or, why didn't the mother's choices still matter more than the child's life after the child was born."

Other than her opposition to abortion, everything else was up for grabs. She continued attending Mass and was still calling herself Catholic, but only because, as she told her friends, she planned to change the Church from the inside out, to help usher it into the modern era. She didn't see it at the time, but, "My pro-life convictions were the roots that kept me from becoming completely unmoored from my Catholic faith."

By the time she finished graduate school, Jen was looking to the future. She knew she wanted marriage and a family, but she was dissatisfied with the men she'd dated. It shocked her to realize it, but it was important to her to marry someone who shared her religious background, even as she employed a cafeteria approach to the Faith.

She joined Catholic online dating sites and met her future husband, Demetrio. He, too, had done some picking and choosing at the Catholic salad bar, but by the time they met they had both started on a road to reversion, though Demetrio was closer to returning to Rome than Jen. Demetrio initially challenged Jen to reconsider positions on several issues. Over time, they pushed and challenged each other as they explored and discussed their faith.

They got engaged, married, and soon their discussions and mutual challenges changed foundational areas of their lives: they realized they needed to add more genuine, frequent prayer to their lives, and they decided not to use contraception. However, in other areas of their lives they were still not fully aligned with the Church.

Three years into their marriage, when a move from New York City to Washington, D.C., left Jen jobless, she reluctantly returned to school and entered another graduate program at the Pontifical John Paul II Institute for Studies on Marriage and Family at The Catholic University of America. Her first semester shocked her. Her peers stunned her with their genuine, joyful love of and devotion to their Catholic faith. The faculty, too, challenged her, both intellectually and morally as:

> ... they argued convincingly and expansively about so many different issues related to faith, reason, human sexuality, American culture, and Western civilization. I began to reexamine practically everything I had taken for granted my entire life. I had already left behind relativism. I knew that truth was an objective reality. Because of this, when faced with their devastating logic and faithful claims, I was forced into a serious place of cognitive dissonance. I felt backed into a corner. I realized that either they're right or I'm right about issue X. It can no longer be both ways.... I could no longer fall back on, "Well, what's right for you isn't right for me."

> It was exhausting and painful to fight myself. One day I finally gave in and admitted I was wrong. I went to confession at the Basilica of the National Shrine of the Immaculate Conception in D.C. (across the street from my classes) and just sobbed to the priest that I had been so wrong and so disobedient for a very long time. I finally began to see submission to Holy Mother Church as a privilege and a gift rather than a burden to be fought. I finally began to see that obedience isn't weakness forced on people who don't know any better, but strength for our journey toward holiness.

I spent two years at the institute, and they remain some of the richest years for me and Demetrio. He began to crave the discussions we'd have about the things I was learning. We read so much about so many difficult topics. God formed our family at our wedding, but God shaped and molded our family (sometimes by fire) through the institute.

Jen and Demetrio don't consider themselves finished products, but if they had to complete a diversity exercise today and answer the question, "Who are you?" now they know exactly what they would say, and it would definitely include a rosary.

Love Overcomes

A lengthy conversion can have its own inner dynamic, like water polishing stone into something brilliant.

Dan and Liz were married for more than forty years before they joined the Catholic Church. Their conversion unfolded bit by bit over the years. Liz—who read the biography of St. Bernadette mentioned in the last chapter—believed, as early as when she was in her twenties, that the Catholic Church was the Church founded by Jesus Christ. Her husband, however, had an aversion to Catholicism, thanks to a former girlfriend's grandmother who had made unreasonable demands on Dan regarding the possibility of conversion.

Dan was so soured on religion that for a long time after they married Liz hid her Bible in a linen closet. With the advent of their first child, however, she grew brave enough to bring her bible into the light and even insisted on baptism for the baby. Dan unenthusiastically agreed.

Liz began raising the children in Protestant traditions, with Dan merely trailing along for the ride. Over the years, Catholics who lived their faith with authenticity and joy made repeated appearances in their lives. Liz could never shake the idea that she wanted to be Catholic and was secretly delighted whenever a new Catholic friend had a positive effect on Dan. When they met and befriended Fr. Will through an ecumenical Bible study, Dan was surprised that he felt so comfortable hanging out with a priest. A beer with Fr. Will was precisely the abbreviated catechism Dan needed at that stage.

Some Catholic neighbors invited the couple to a Christians Encounter Christ (CEC) weekend. Initially, Dan and Liz said no, but after repeated invitations they gave in. They loved the experience and started attending Catholic Bible studies. They volunteered to help with CEC weekends. Dan was finding his clan, though the couple continued to attend a Protestant church.

Liz became friends with a woman who was a Benedictine oblate, and she was so drawn to Benedictine spirituality that she became an oblate, too. Her friend suggested getting some spiritual direction, and that was when Liz met Sister Marie Therese. Sister Marie's honesty, down-to-earth style, and deep love for Jesus mesmerized Liz.

As the Protestant church they'd been attending grew fuzzier in its theology, Dan and Liz felt more and more adrift. They had grown to love and appreciate Christian community. Dan turned to Liz in frustration one day and said: "What do we do now? Where do we *go*?"

"It seems pretty obvious to me," Liz said. "The Catholic Church."

They were received into the Church when Liz was sixty-seven and Dan was seventy-two years old.

"Love overcomes, love delights, those who love the Sacred Heart rejoice."

—St. Bernadette Soubirous[28]

Faith and Reason

Owen, a scientist and an old friend from college, was the last man I dreamed would convert to Catholicism, but then he probably thought the same of Tom and me.

We reconnected a few years ago on Facebook, and one day I noticed that Owen often "liked" some of my specifically Catholic status updates. Hmmm, I wondered, what does he think of the fact that Tom and I are Catholic? Is he just being polite?

One day, after posting a story on my blog about Tom's conversion, Owen dropped a bombshell in the form of a comment: Many years after abandoning her Catholic faith, his wife had returned to it, and Owen was now planning to start RCIA in the fall. My response was something eloquent and articulate like, "*Wow!*"

Owen grew up in a household I could identify with. His father professed no religion and his mother, though Jewish, did not practice her faith. Owen remembers going to church only twice in his childhood, with a friend. As a young man, he was drawn to philosophy and Eastern religion, particularly through the Tao Te Ching. When he took a college course in world religions the ritual of the Catholic Church intrigued him, but his vague attraction didn't blossom. A scientist with a solid understanding of how the physical world works, Owen believed that his questions about the nature of the universe were basically settled.

However, he started feeling less certain that science could explain everything he wanted to know. He said he began "questioning the 'why' and 'to what end,' which science cannot answer. It has left a void that I am unable to fill with secular humanism, empty political rhetoric, or material things."

When Owen's wife started watching daily Mass on EWTN, Owen was curious. It would take almost no time out of his day, he reasoned, so he sat down to view it with her. After watching for a week, he was yearning to watch the Holy Sacrifice of the Mass every day:

It gave me an indescribable peace that I hadn't felt in years. The next step was easy—I went to the local Catholic church to determine if I felt the same way. I did. Catholicism provides me with answers to questions to which I have never found an adequate answer. My wife's witness to me, as she discovers how her return to the faith has changed her outlook and attitudes, has been a wonder to behold and has affected me deeply.

One-Hundred Percent Entrusted

Sometimes, stages of conversion proceed smoothly, minus pain and anxiety, and with great trust. As a young woman, my friend Danae—the one who was so impressed by Fr. Joe's love for Jesus—firmly believed that she wanted to marry a man who was strong in his Catholic faith. However, after dating Karl, a non-Catholic, for a while, she realized he was the person she wanted to spend the rest of her life with. Karl felt the same way. They started talking about marriage. Danae says:

> The idea of him becoming Catholic was never seriously talked about. We had an understanding that he would remain Presbyterian and I would remain Catholic and that we would go to both churches every Sunday. I always prayed that God's will be done, and that God would reveal things to Karl in his own way. I was very clear about non-negotiables for me such as natural family planning and raising children Catholic.

> Whenever a big difference came up, we talked about it (sometimes fought about it), and I usually pointed him in the direction of some resources, but then I left it alone,

which is *not* my style! By nature I am a wound-picker because I always want to resolve conflict immediately. But I just entrusted this to the Lord.

I think because Karl was always so drawn to liturgy, I knew God was going to draw him into the Church. It is the one area in my life where I one-hundred percent entrusted something to the Lord without worry. Karl did, through reading and prayer, come to the understanding that the Catholic Church was the true Church, and once he knew that, he wanted to become Catholic as quickly as possible.

Not only was Karl received into the Church, he is now a music and liturgy director for one of the largest Catholic parishes in Nebraska.

Labyrinthine Ways

It's often impossible to identify what stage of conversion someone is in. Sometimes there is visible progress, but most of the time we're just guessing. In the midst of hoping for someone, especially someone we love, to convert, we get impatient. "Is he close? Will she come to Mass with me *now*? When will she make the leap? Why won't he talk about confession?" But we shouldn't give up or get discouraged. When I consider how messy and unpredictable my own conversion was, I ask: "Who am I to give up on anyone else? What right do I have to write off the soul of another?"

Galsworthy was right about messy beginnings, but I would add that the middle of a conversion is messy, too. And even endings aren't tidy, because conversion is a process that doesn't end until we die. The "ending" of a conversion period is really just another beginning. As St. Francis de Sales said:

We must be patient and little by little root out our bad inclinations, overcome our aversions, and control our emotions. This life is truly a continual warfare, and there is no one who can say, "I am never tempted." Peace is reserved for heaven, where the palm of victory awaits us; on earth there is a continual struggle between hope and fear. However, our hope must be strong, relying on the omnipotence of God, who is always ready to help us. So never tire of fighting for your growth and perfection.[29]

Tom, me, Jack, Holly, Karl, Danae, Owen and his wife, Jen, Demetrio, Liz, Dan, Meg, her husband … we are all plot points on an enormous map of conversion and only the Lord can see both the rocky terrain and the final destination. We can all learn from Danae's words and approach: "It is the one area in my life where I one-hundred percent entrusted something to the Lord without worry."

We can trust the Hound of Heaven.

CHAPTER 7

Don't Lose Patience:
Hope for the Married

WHAT'S IT LIKE WHEN ONE SPOUSE wants to make a leap and the other looks askance at or is horrified by the chasm? I wish there were a definitive answer to the question, "What do I do when my spouse rejects the path I'm taking?" Because I know how challenging that is for the "unequally yoked," I'd love to say, "Just follow my five-step plan, and you, too, can have a converted spouse in ninety days!" But there are no five-step plans.

Therefore, my only advice sounds, as most advice does, lame and ineffective at first, but it's all I've got. Pray. And be patient and loving. Pray. And talk, don't yell. Pray. And respect your spouse. Pray. Follow the Lord's promptings and don't force your faith on your spouse. Pray. And don't lose hope or patience. Detecting a pattern? It's in God's hands, not ours.

Not What He Bargained For

My husband married a nice atheist girl. He never envisioned himself married to a Christian, and most certainly not to a Catholic Christian. We laugh about it now, but a few years into our marriage, when I was investigating Christianity, I asked Tom what he would think if I became Christian. He said: "That's fine with me. Just so it doesn't affect my life."

Given that (a) Tom married a pro-choice atheist who didn't want children and considered Christianity sexist garbage, and (b) I'm now a home-schooling, Catholic mom with three daughters on earth and five babies in heaven, I think we can safely say that (c) Tom's life has changed.

I did my best to be sympathetic to the fact that Tom never signed up for this twisted set of events. I'd been a baptized Christian, courtesy of an obliging Episcopal priest when I was thirty, five years before I was received into the Catholic Church. It was another five years before Tom came into the Church, so for ten years (actually more than ten years, since I didn't reach the decision for baptism overnight), I tried to follow my own advice with my spouse.

When Tom did make the decision to be received into the Church, it was swift and definite, and just weeks before the Easter Vigil. I saw it coming but was simultaneously stunned that it was actually happening. One thing I had accepted, though, in the not-too-distant past: the decision was not mine. This conversion business was between God and Tom, and I had no control over any of it.

Epiphany

For the longest time, I thought I would be the only spiritual seeker in my marriage.

I had come to God slowly, in stages that were visible to me only in hindsight. I had come to him through years of interrogating my believing friends. I had come to him by way of searching, yearning, praying. I had met him in the pages of books, thanks to writers such as George MacDonald and C. S. Lewis.

One night, I was reading Lewis's *Mere Christianity*. When I read that God "hates the sin, but loves the sinner" I was confounded. How could God separate what I had done from who I am? I had been guilty of what Christianity described as terrible sins. Could God *really* love me after all that I had done?

As Lewis's words sank in, I had an epiphany. I realized that I loved others in the way Lewis described. I was capable of continuing to love people who had hurt me—I didn't dismiss them as composites of their bad behavior. They were just human beings, guilty of hurtful acts or stupid choices, as I had been, but they were not caricatures of evil. That, Lewis was saying, was exactly how God loved me.

For as long as I could remember, I'd thought my actions defined me. To condemn my actions as evil meant condemning myself as evil. It's a dilemma many struggle with when facing conversion. I'd made a leap and finally accepted that certain acts and positions were objectively wrong, but where did that leave me? If my actions were sinful, everything about me must be sinful, unacceptable, and shameful.

For years, in order to continue thinking of myself as the good and compassionate person I assumed myself to be, I'd subconsciously justified my actions. I experienced the same kind of cognitive dissonance that Jen mentioned: trying to hold on to conflicting beliefs or mesh two disparate ways of thinking and being. It was an indescribable relief to embrace a new way of seeing myself in relationship to God. If God could separate what I had done from who I was, maybe I could, too.

I remembered something Jack had said to me years before. "Someday, Karen," he said, "you will realize that you are not the sum of your actions." His words must have taken root but lain dormant for a long time. Now they were breaking through the surface. Maybe I was not garbage to be bagged up and left by the curb. Maybe the sins were the garbage?

I literally dropped to my knees and sobbed. I asked God's forgiveness—so many sins, for such a long time. I felt hope for the first time in years. When Tom got home from work that night, I cried in his arms as I tried to explain my realization.

I wasn't ready to call myself a Christian but I thought maybe I could call myself a theist, as Lewis had done at a certain point in his conversion. A deist? I wasn't sure. But I knew I believed in something, and I knew that the "something" could conceivably love me.

Slowly, my faith grew. Jack patiently coached from the sidelines, offering encouragement and an understanding ear when I needed it. I came to Jesus in small steps, through movement that is fatal for a questioner: reading Scripture, praying, asking Christ, if he was truly God, to reveal himself to me. I gazed on a sublime crucifix in Jack's church and, even though I was still convinced I could never become a Catholic, ached to feel something for the man on the cross. And one day that man answered my prayer. Imperceptibly, he drew me closer, until one day when I had to admit—to myself and to God—that I believed, not only in "a god" but in Jesus Christ.

I was still uncomfortable calling myself a Christian, but I knew one thing: it was time to find others who could help me take the next step. It was time to start shopping. Where does a new believer go to find a church that fits?

Not All Who Wander Are Lost

I started with a Lutheran church, which seemed a sensible place to begin, given Tom's background, and attended four months of weekly meetings with the pastor. We read the Bible together and he assigned books for me to read, including several on Martin Luther. I found that I disagreed with much of the theology and decided to move on. I lamented: "If only my beloved C. S. Lewis had started a church, I'd join! I wish I could be a Lewisian!" But soft, what denominational light through yonder window breaks? Lewis was a member of the Church of England! I could at least brush up against the C. of E. by way of the Episcopal church in my humble little Nebraska town.

I hunted down the nearest one—twenty miles away. I still remember feeling enveloped by the place the first time I walked into St. Matthew's. The church was warm and lovely, with a welcoming pastor. It offered me the ritual, liturgy, and weekly communion I'd come to crave and had none of the things I found distasteful about the Catholic Church. I wasn't ready to formally join this or any other denomination, but for a while I felt at home.

Tom and I had been married for six years. His formerly atheist wife was now calling herself a Christian and scheduling a baptism with an Episcopalian priest. These were strange days indeed. Tom witnessed my baptism—and Jack drove five hundred miles to be there—but that was as far as Tom's support could go. He had no interest in my new church.

It was my turn to be as patient with my husband as my friend had been with me. In my first months as a baptized Christian, Tom and I had a lot of adjustments to make. Our leisurely Sundays with coffee and the newspaper were upended as I hustled out of the house to get to church. We had tense arguments, and then came the most enormous upheaval since my conversion: I wanted to have a baby. I explained to my dazed husband that it seemed the natural next step in a Christian marriage, but this was too much. Tom rejected my proposal. Children were not part of the bargain.

I prayed in earnest that Tom would one day agree to have a child. I have no explanation (aside from miracles) for the fact that within a year Tom's heart softened. I went off the pill and became pregnant easily, but we had two consecutive miscarriages. As we shared our grief, we grew closer, and Tom started going to church with me. I was happy he was going but was unsure about what he believed. When the priest asked if we were ready to join the Episcopal church, Tom shocked me by saying yes. I wasn't ready. I still had so many questions about the divisions in Christianity, but I went ahead with confirmation because I longed for spiritual unity with my husband. Only later would I find out that Tom had gone through with it solely for my sake.

The following year, we had our first baby but also headed into serious marital difficulties as we faced down some of the demons of our past. We both stopped attending the Episcopal church. I was sad and adrift. After Jack suggested I pray the Chaplet of Divine Mercy, some of Tom's and my problems seemed to resolve, miraculously again. I tentatively took that as a sign to look into Catholicism. I didn't think the chaplet was a magic charm, but *something* was going on. I still had endless questions about Catholicism, but, two years later, the night would arrive when I could say with utter conviction the words, "I believe and profess all that the holy Catholic Church believes, teaches, and proclaims to be revealed by God."

The Easter Vigil

The night I was received into the Church, I was alone.

That's not entirely accurate. Jack was there and so was my sponsor. Carolyn and I first met at the RCIA meeting where she was assigned to me. *A stranger for a sponsor, how weird is this?* I'd thought. *The whole class must feel sorry for me.* I'd wanted Jack to sponsor me, but a weekly two-hour drive for RCIA was impractical, so I accepted the sponsorship of a generous stranger.

Jack drove up for the Easter Vigil and brought along a friend to keep him company for the four hours he would be on the road that night. Tom stayed home with our toddler. He didn't want to prevent me from becoming Catholic, but he didn't want to be in on it, either. Carolyn, Jack, and someone I barely knew. *How weird is this?* I thought. *I am pathetic.*

At the Vigil Mass, fear and awe mingled with an odd detachment and observation of what was happening. In the middle of the Mass an usher tapped me on the shoulder and asked me to help carry the gifts forward to the priest. I trembled as I carried the decanter of wine. *This is going to become the precious Blood of Jesus,* I thought, *and I will consume him—Body, Blood, Soul, and Divinity. And I am alone.*

No, not alone! I scolded. *Jack is here, all these people are here. God is here!* But I couldn't deny the fact that my husband was not there.

When I received holy Communion for the first time, I wasn't transported to a new plane, as I had secretly hoped I would be. Something I desperately longed for was missing—spiritual unity with my husband. And yet I suddenly felt ... what? Grounded. Firm. Certain. I didn't have a single regret about what I was doing. I wasn't sure how I could feel quiet exultation and deep sadness at the same time, but I did, because I realized now, down to my bones, this: I was *not* alone.

I walked out of my first Easter Vigil knowing that despite my sadness over my husband's absence, I had a steadfast companion. Jesus would not let me down.

A Shower of Roses

I became active in my parish as an RCIA sponsor, then a team member, speaker, and teacher. I made new Catholic friends, and joined Bible studies but I attended Mass alone most of the time. Tom and I shared nothing of this new part of my life, and it pained us both that the new core of my existence created a chasm between us.

I'd been a Catholic for three years when I started seeing Fr. Joe for monthly spiritual direction. One bright spring day, he suggested that he and I both pray to St. Thérèse of Lisieux for Tom's conversion. "Look for a sign of roses," Fr. Joe told me.

About a month later, Tom and I were sitting in the backyard of the house we'd bought the previous summer. Tom had been laboring to get the overgrown yard in shape, ruthlessly chopping, cutting, and trimming. As we sat outside that evening, chatting and enjoying the pleasant, warm weather and watching our little daughters play, Tom glanced over toward the greenery that was next to the house.

"Well, look at that!" he exclaimed. "That's a rose bush!" My heart leapt as I looked in the direction he'd indicated.

"I almost chopped that down the other day," he said casually. "I didn't realize it was a rose bush. I don't know what stopped me, but for some reason, I thought I should leave it there."

I was speechless. I got up to more closely examine the delicate pink rosebuds that were whispering "Miracle, miracle!" to me. I dared to hope these roses were a sign of something happening in Tom's heart. I prayed silently, thanking St. Thérèse for her encouragement. When Fr. Joe came to dinner the following week, St. Thérèse's roses were on the dinner table.

I was still working with RCIA. It was time consuming, but I loved it. In fact, I loved it so much that when I began to hear God calling me away from it, I wanted to stick my fingers in my ears. He couldn't possibly want me to stop this good work, could he? But a nagging voice kept saying: "Pull back from witnessing to others and witness in your own home. Show Tom that your love for him and your family is the most important thing in your world."

With a heavy heart I resigned from the team. When Holy Week rolled around that year, it was strange to be home with my husband on Holy Thursday instead of participating in the gorgeous Mass I'd come to love. Instead of being absorbed in frantic, last-minute RCIA prep, I was home, calm, and present to my family. I spent the evening with my two little girls, creating a "Holy Family meal" and coloring pictures of the Last Supper. My five-year-old built a crucifix out of blocks and showed it to her daddy. On Holy Saturday night, instead of being out late for the Vigil Mass with people Tom didn't know, I was home with him. Our family went to Mass together on Easter Sunday.

I was expecting another baby, too. After our second child, Tom had declared we were "done." But months of novenas to St. Joseph seemed to bring another miracle. Tom was open to more children. We were devastated when, a month after Easter, we lost the baby. Earlier that winter, before I was pregnant, a dear friend of mine told me she had a recurring feeling that Tom and I would conceive a son, and that our son would somehow lead Tom to the Church. I seriously doubted this; Tom was still stubbornly resistant. But from the moment I became pregnant, I felt that I was carrying a baby boy. After the miscarriage, we named our baby James Matthias, and I asked our son to intercede for his father.

Just three months later, Tom and I sat up late one night talking. He said he'd been thinking about the nature of evil, about how it really comes down to being separated from God. "And," he said slowly, "I don't think I want to be separated anymore. I want to be where you and the girls are." His words took my breath away.

He still didn't want to be Catholic but asked if he could sit in on the RCIA classes that were starting in September, "just to learn more, not to join the Church," he insisted. I rejoined the RCIA team that fall, and the director let Tom be an unofficial participant. When the candidates and catechumens went through the Rite of Welcoming and Acceptance, Tom did not participate. "Not gonna join," he said. Through that winter, he listened, talked, questioned, read, and thought. And he took my advice about one thing. I asked him to try a simple prayer: "God, if you're there, let me know." In addition to the things we discussed at RCIA and at home, Tom was pondering his beliefs about music, art, and the nature of beauty. His conviction that there is objective beauty was leading him to consider the possibility of objective truth about God and the nature of the universe.

Fr. Joe was an influence, too. He was a regular dinner guest at our home, and Tom was surprised and impressed by Father's mix of intelligence, spirituality, warmth, and humor. I prayed (and asked Fr. Joe and St. Thérèse to join me) that Tom would come into the Church before our oldest daughter's first holy Communion.

By January, Tom was still just an observer and had taken no formal steps. Whenever I asked about it, he said he didn't know exactly what was holding him back, other than fear. I sympathized with the fear of turning into someone unrecognizable, and I told him about a point in my conversion where I knew that I had to make the leap or turn my back. He nodded, and I left it alone.

I was pregnant again, but miscarried again. God granted untold graces through that time of loss, giving me peace and an acceptance of his will that I could scarcely believe and that I could only hope was some kind of witness to Tom.

While I was in the hospital, after the surgical procedure following that miscarriage, I was struggling to come out of the anesthesia. Tom was by my side, holding my hand, and I remember feeling that I was somehow trying to get back to him as I swam in and out of consciousness. I couldn't fully wake up so I began praying the Rosary, asking the Blessed Mother to help me. And I asked Mary to pray for Tom and his conversion.

I asked the child I had just lost (later we named her Rachel) to pray for her daddy. Alternating decades of the rosary with simple pleas for Tom's soul, I felt a powerful, circular connection among us all—Tom, me, the mother of Our Lord, and Rachel. Though I was physically holding only Tom's hand, it felt as if the Blessed Mother and our daughter were holding tightly to Tom and me, too.

That same month, at Mass, Tom had found that by sitting in the first or second pew he could hear the priest or extraordinary minister of holy Communion saying "Body of Christ" to each communicant. He confided that the repetition of those words had one day helped him enter a deeper state of prayer than he had ever experienced. The next week we were in the front pew, but he couldn't hear anything. He was frustrated, and began to pray, "Please let me hear it again, please let me feel that again." Suddenly, a minister stepped directly in front of him and he heard the words ringing: "The Body of Christ ... the Body of Christ ... the Body of Christ...." When he told me about it, I said, "Tom! Do you see how directly he answered your prayer?" It was, he admitted, "coincidental."

Shortly after that, a friend at RCIA asked Tom, "What's holding you back? I don't get it! You live the Catholic life. You go to Mass, you use NFP, you're there! What is it?" Tom shrugged.

On a Saturday morning just before Lent we woke up at the same time and lay in bed, chatting. Tom asked if I knew the name of the man born blind, from the Gospel of John. He said, "If I joined the Church, that man's name would be my confirmation name." I held my breath for a moment. Could this be happening?

Fr. Joe came to dinner that night and asked the question Tom must have gotten tired of hearing: "So, where are you? What, if anything, is holding you back?"

This time Tom's answer was different. "Nothing," he said. "I'm ready. Can we schedule something?"

The day before Ash Wednesday, we had a private Rite of Welcoming at daily Mass, with Fr. Joe presiding. I acted as Tom's sponsor and during the portion of that rite, in which the sponsor "signs the senses" of the candidate, Tom and I experienced a rebirth in our marriage. We stood before a priest, made promises, professed faith. We committed to God and one another. Our marriage by a judge, sixteen years before, seemed as if it had happened in another lifetime.

Tom proceeded through Lent participating in all that the other RCIA candidates did. Now that he'd made the decision to join the Church, he couldn't wait to get to his first confession. At the Easter Vigil Tom was confirmed and received his first holy Communion. Jack and Holly were there as were Catholic friends who had become Tom's friends, too. Tom hadn't known about the host of prayers sent forth on his behalf, but that night, many who had prayed for him were present, sharing our joy and surprising Tom by telling him how long he'd been cradled in God's love.

A Future and a Hope

There were so many times when I had no idea what God would do next. When our marriage was strained and difficult, I couldn't see through the dark tunnel to the light at the end. I had to walk in blindness until the Lord led me to the next stop, but that's what faith is—a series of steps in the dark and wholehearted trust that my Guide won't let me fall.

I cherished this Scripture from the Book of Isaiah: "I will lead the blind in a way that they know not, in paths that they have not known I will guide them. I will turn the darkness before them into light, the rough places into level ground" (42:16). Now, when I am tempted to give up hope or lose patience, I remember that God was at work, guiding me in one instance after another. When I converted alone, lacked unity with my husband, left a ministry I loved, lost arguments, lost every sense of firm footing, God was there. When I lost babies, thought my husband would never consider Catholicism, felt utterly alone, God was there. Through quiet exultation and deep sadness, with every stumbling step, my Lord cradled me in his love.

Not every story ends as mine did, and, in truth, our story was just beginning. Sometimes one spouse converts and the other never does. I know men and women who are still waiting, still hoping. Every soul is a deep mystery. I don't know why things happen in some lives and not in others, but the bottom line is the same. The advice might sound weak and ineffective at first, but it's all we've got this side of heaven, so I'll repeat it:

Pray. And be patient and loving. Pray. And talk, don't yell. Pray. And respect your spouse. Pray. Follow the Lord's promptings and don't force your faith on your spouse. Pray. And don't lose hope or patience. Leave your spouse in God's capable hands.

"For I know the plans I have for you, says the Lord, plans for welfare and not for evil, to give you a future and a hope."

—Jeremiah 29:11

CHAPTER 8

Don't Forget That Words Matter

"Some say it is unreasonable to be courteous
and gentle with a reckless person who insults
you for no reason at all. I have made a pact with
my tongue; not to speak when my heart is dis-
turbed."

—St. Francis de Sales[30]

MAGGIE SAT AT THE DINING ROOM TABLE with her mother-in-law,
Marcia, and her sister-in-law, Eileen.

"It's disgusting," said Marcia. "I can't imagine what kind of person could do it. How do they live with themselves?"

"I know!" said Eileen. "It's selfish and it's murder, plain and
simple. I don't know how anyone could call it anything else."

Maggie sipped her coffee and wondered how to excuse herself
from the conversation without seeming rude.

"I mean, right, Maggie?" asked Eileen, turning to her. "It's not
just a 'choice.' I don't understand how people justify it." She looked
at Maggie expectantly.

"Yeah," murmured Maggie, "I dunno." She shrugged and
looked into her coffee cup, as if it might offer her some magical
escape route. She took another sip and said, "What are they watching in the living room?"

"Well, it's a *selfish* choice," said Marcia, ignoring Maggie's attempt at diversion. "They're all about 'choice' this and 'choice' that, but what they really want is to make their own selfish choices." She shook her head. "They're just awful."

"Would you excuse me?" said Maggie. "I just need to run to the restroom," she said, getting up from the table.

"Oh, sure honey," said Marcia, who turned back to Eileen. "When they find themselves in hell," Marcia said as Maggie started out of the room, "they won't be so keen on the choices that landed them there."

In the bathroom, Maggie leaned on the counter and looked at herself in the mirror. *What would they think if they knew? What would they say if they realized they were talking about me?*

Her abortion had been several years ago. She'd been desperate, with no idea how she could have supported a baby. She felt stupid to have even gotten pregnant, wished she'd used more reliable birth control. There was no way she could have a child. She'd been alone and terrified about the future. Everyone she knew—her parents, friends, nearly everyone—believed abortion was a reasonable solution to an unplanned pregnancy. A modern, civilized, sensible option. Only religious fanatics objected to it. So Maggie had taken what she thought was the responsible way out of her problem.

The father had supported her decision. "It's your body," he said, "it should be your decision." Now, years later, Maggie was married. She couldn't imagine ever telling her sweet, pro-life in-laws about the sad, desperate choice she'd once made. Maggie wondered, sometimes, about Christianity, even considered learning more about it, but when moments like this one arose—when her Christian in-laws talked about "those women"—she didn't know what to do.

She'd struggled after her abortion, experienced regret. She had even begun to wonder if abortion was intrinsically wrong, that not only had *she* made a terrible choice, but that it was a choice *no one* should ever make. How could she discuss any of that with her new family? They would hate her if they knew. It almost made her dig in her pro-choice heels, to defiantly, adamantly, defend her choice all over again.

Hard Battles

"Pain insists upon being attended to," C. S. Lewis said. "God whispers to us in our pleasures, speaks in our consciences, but shouts in our pains. It is his megaphone to rouse a deaf world."[31] A mortal sin, precisely because of the pain it causes, can become the first herald of repentance. A sin that causes immense regret, as abortion does, can be used by the Lord as his megaphone to rouse a deaf soul. In the minefield that is conversion, converts need to be able to find safe spaces and know that Christians genuinely care about what they're going through, that we understand their confusion and fear. Reexamining everything one has ever believed is overwhelming and frightening.

Catholics who have grown up with the doctrines of the Church have the privilege of seeing the world through a clear lens that brings natural law, objective right and wrong, sin, contrition, sacrifice, and redemption into focus. But one who hasn't grown up that way sees the world through a cloud. The purpose of life, the practice of religion, certain "rules and regulations" are fuzzy and out of focus for people who grow up, as I did, piecing their beliefs together from the secular world.

In our attempts to share the Faith, it's helpful to remember a couple of things. First, evangelization is not a solo flight. We can and always should call on the Holy Spirit to help us navigate our interactions. A short mental prayer, such as "Come, Holy Spirit!" is invaluable and reminds us that conversion is not our work, but God's.

Second, charity is a virtue often spoken of but too often neglected. Many of the people we encounter every day are living vastly different realities from our own, and have never really been presented with the Gospel. The presumption that others know the truth but have rejected it can tempt us to lead with defensiveness. That tone, however, especially when it precedes friendship, can result in hurt feelings or short-circuit any possibility of genuinely sharing the Gospel.

I'm not advocating a lifelong walk on eggshells, nor am I suggesting that we harbor a crippling fear of offending others. But it's important to consider that others are entitled to the same respect, sensitivity, and benefit of the doubt that we would like. Erring on the side of charity is never a bad idea. "Be kind" goes a popular saying, "for everyone you meet is fighting a hard battle."

In Lewis's *The Horse and His Boy*, we're reminded of how little we are privy to the hidden pain in the heart of another. Aslan speaks:

> "I was the lion who forced you to join with Aravis. I was the cat who comforted you among the houses of the dead. I was the lion who drove the jackals from you while you slept. I was the lion who gave the horses the new strength of fear for the last mile so that you should reach King Lune in time. And I was the lion you do not remember who pushed the boat in which you lay, a child near death, so that it came to shore where a man sat, wakeful at night, to receive you."

> "Then it was you who wounded Aravis?"

> "It was I."

> "But what for?"

> "Child," said the Voice, "I am telling you your story, not hers. I tell no one any story but his own."

Do They Know?

As a convert, I was shown again and again by charitable Christians that they loved me even when they profoundly disagreed with my ideas and actions or found them to be immoral. I strive now to live up to the tender models of charity that my friends were to me. Sometimes opportunities pop up in the most unexpected places.

Years ago, I joined a group in my parish for mothers of young children. I was chatting one day with one of the other moms, a woman I did not yet know very well, but liked, and we seemed to have a lot in common. She was serious about her faith and about being the best Catholic mom she could be. I had recently had a miscarriage, and we somehow got started talking about it. As we discussed loss, infertility, and the struggle to have children, she told me about a friend of hers who had just undergone an *in vitro* fertilization (IVF) procedure.

"Would you ever do that?" she asked. "I mean, I know miscarriage isn't the same kind of infertility problem, but if it came to that?"

I was taken aback, surprised at her implication that IVF was an acceptable route for a Catholic. *Maybe*, I thought, *she just doesn't know?*

"Well," I ventured, formulating my response carefully, "personally, I could never do something that was against Church teaching. So *I* wouldn't pursue that route. I genuinely feel for your friend, though. I totally understand how the desire for a baby leads someone to look into extraordinary means. It's so painful to not be able to have a child."

My new friend was shocked: "IVF is against Church teaching? *Why?*"

I actually felt relieved. She *didn't* know. This wasn't an argument waiting to happen, and I didn't have to gear up for a debate. She had simply been lacking in facts. We talked in more detail about it and I explained the reasoning behind the Church's position. As our friendship grew, discussion of the faith remained an integral part of it.

The Catholic Way

It's not just in doctrinal issues and moral discussions that words (and presumptions) matter. Sometimes, as Catholics, we have fixed ideas about the Catholic way of doing things. That can lead to our assumption that we know more of another person's story than we do.

In my book *After Miscarriage*, I shared a story about family size. Many of us subconsciously think of "good" Catholic families as large families. Because Tom and I have had so many miscarriages, our larger family is not visible to the world, and I have occasionally run into people who notice the number of visible children and make assumptions. Such assumptions can be painful for someone who has experienced infertility or the loss of children. Questions such as "Just the three kids?" aren't meant to hurt, but they can rub salt in the wound, especially if the wound is raw and recent.

Years ago, just two weeks after I'd had my fifth miscarriage, I was at a gathering and met a friend's mother. She asked if I had children. At the time I had two and I proudly shared my daughters' names and ages. She nodded politely then turned to the woman next to me, who said she had five children. My friend's mother broke into an enormous smile. "That's *wonderful!*" she gushed. "So few people have that many these days!"

She didn't mean to be unkind, but I was devastated. Feeling fragile and defective, I wanted to shout, "I have more babies in heaven—don't they *count?*" She had no idea what I'd been through and, of course, it was not the time or place to recount my losses, so I said nothing. But her words, born of an assumption, stung.

There was nothing wrong with her enthusiastic support for large families—and I know large families endure more than their share of insensitive remarks—but the undercurrent that afternoon was that someone who had "only two" children might be guilty of doing something "less than Catholic."

The Issue Is Not the Issue

Let's go back to Maggie. Abortion is one of those hot-button topics that we all encounter, so let's look at how our words can help or hurt when we're evangelizing for life.

From my years in the pro-choice camp I know that many pro-choice people maintain their positions because they've either had an abortion or love someone who has. In their minds, "killing" doesn't define what they or their loved ones are capable of. Therefore, they reason, abortion cannot be murder. They are grappling with the same kind of cognitive dissonance I had before I grasped that God could hate my sins but still love me. Perhaps because of my own conversion, I am especially sensitive to people in this position. I remember, after several years as a Catholic and as a supporter of pro-life causes, hearing the expression "pro-aborts" from a priest. I shuddered. I still have friends and family who are pro-choice, and they are not the hardhearted people he presumed them to be. I longed for a way to convey that they are compassionate people whose compassion has been misdirected.

When talking to pro-choice friends and relatives, understand that they see their position, as I once saw mine, as loving and supportive of women in crisis pregnancies. Acknowledging that compassion and building on it is more helpful than labeling someone a murderer. Many who call themselves pro-choice are personally opposed to abortion, but they aren't sure how to navigate that position socially or politically. When we call them "baby killers" and "murderers," we effectively shut down the conversation.

And precisely because so many pro-choice adherents have been personally touched by abortion, remind yourself that you're not dealing with reason and logic alone, but with strong personal feelings. We may think we're having a theoretical or political discussion, but in reality we may be talking to someone who is facing down sin, shame, and confusion. With more than 57 million abortions since 1973, what are the chances that you *don't* know someone who has been personally involved in an abortion? It could be your next-door neighbor, your best friend, that nice lady at the bakery, the young man who goes to school with your daughter, your grandmother, your teacher, your FedEx delivery guy, your student, your daughter-in-law.

And so, the issue—in this case, abortion is the taking of a human life—isn't always the issue. The real issue might be, "Abortion brought immense pain into my life and I don't know what to do about it." So tread lightly. Our words matter, and so does our mercy and compassion.

My own conversion from abortion supporter to advocate for life was a long process. In my youth, I'd adopted the cultural view of sex that I saw around me: sex was a given. So was birth control. And if birth control failed, abortion was sometimes necessary for women to retain their freedom and autonomy.

Over the years, Jack helped me sift through all of this because he was willing to simply talk without condemning me. Early on he thought that if he could convince me life begins at conception he would win the argument. But he was facing bigger opposition than that. I embodied a pervasive, powerful worldview about sex and its meaning.

Over time our conversations led me to the truth that abortion takes a life, but I still defined my position in a very elementary way: "If you do get pregnant, don't have an abortion." It took me much longer to examine the ramifications of birth control and to reach the point where I believed that sex was meant only for marriage. That represented a seismic mental shift. Given my long-held philosophies, it seemed primitive, prudish, or almost nonsensical to say such a thing. Yet I finally believed it mattered deeply that sex creates new human beings, and that the people who create a new being have a responsibility to it. This new belief about sex was scary, and it was pivotal to my conversion to Catholicism.

It was only through ongoing conversations with a dear friend that I reached this point. For a long time, Jack and I weren't even talking about the same thing, but gentle conversations helped me sort through years of assumptions and, eventually, my heart was changed.

Who Has Condemned You?

Recently, I got together for coffee with a friend I hadn't seen in a number of years. Paige has been struggling with her Catholic upbringing, particularly because she has a sister and friends who are gay. She is supportive of their lifestyle and isn't sure how to reconcile her acceptance of gay relationships with returning to the Catholic Church. She asked me to explain the Church's position on homosexuality. I did my best to clarify that the Church respects the dignity of every human being and that the teachings on same-sex attraction are part of a whole, integrated, and beautiful approach to human sexuality. She listened thoughtfully and respectfully but said that she just didn't agree.

Our coffee date did not change my friend's mind, but I didn't expect it to. The point I hoped to share with her was on a slightly more personal note. For me, becoming a Catholic was not about finding a church that meshed with the things I already believed. Becoming a Catholic was about a search for truth, and the search became immensely uncomfortable when truth conflicted with my long-held views

Remember the Scripture about the woman caught in adultery? The Gospel of John recounts the time the Pharisees bring a woman to Jesus, claiming she is guilty of adultery and should be stoned. Jesus doesn't speak to them, but bends to the ground and writes in the dirt with his finger. The Pharisees ask him again—should she not be stoned? Then Jesus challenges the one among them who is without sin to throw the first stone. One by one, they walk away:

> Jesus looked up and said to her, "Woman, where are they? Has no one condemned you?" She said, "No one, Lord." And Jesus said, "Neither do I condemn you; go, and do not sin again" (8:10-11).

In refusing to condemn her Jesus was not telling the woman that her actions were objectively acceptable and that she could continue doing what she'd been doing. As St. John Paul II said (emphasis added):

> This Gospel passage clearly teaches that Christian forgiveness is not synonymous with mere tolerance, but implies something more demanding. It does not mean overlooking evil, or even worse, denying it. God does not forgive evil *but the individual, and he teaches us to distinguish the evil act, which as such must be condemned, from the person who has committed it, to whom he offers the possibility of changing.*
>
> While man tends to identify the sinner with his sin, closing every escape, the heavenly Father instead has sent his Son into the world to offer everyone a way to salvation.[32]

Pope Benedict XVI continued the same theme, stressing:

> Jesus does not enter into a theoretical discussion with his interlocutors on this section of Mosaic Law; he is not concerned with winning an academic dispute about an inter-

pretation of Mosaic Law, but his goal is to save a soul and reveal that salvation is only found in God's love.[33]

Jesus told the woman what she needed to do, offered his grace, and then he left the next step up to her.

We're called to speak in love to our family, friends, and neighbors, and to invite them into this incredible home we've found, the Church. But how will they ever come near the front door if we don't give them a chance to question and if we don't answer with lovingly chosen words? It's hard to convince others that God loves them if we can't speak the words that prove we love them, too.

One of my favorite passages about word battles appears in Madeleine L'Engle's autobiographical book, *A Circle of Quiet*. Though it's regarding a benign subject, the exchange speaks volumes. L'Engle recounts an argument about baseball between her husband and ten-year-old son.

Bion said, "But, Daddy, you just don't understand!"

Hugh replied in his reasonable way, "It's not that I don't understand. I just don't agree with you."

To which our son returned, "If you don't agree with me, you don't understand."[34]

For most of us, it's easy to communicate that way—we talk past each other and look for easy agreement rather than understanding. Too often, instead of calmly discussing opposing viewpoints, we yell, then walk away in anger or disgust, or click out of Facebook after posting a particularly pithy remark. We cut conversations off in the heat of the moment, as if hearts and minds could be changed over one cup of coffee. But conversion is a process, not a moment, so we must keep talking. No matter what we're discussing we must use words that build, strengthen, and help us sort through the issues—and see when the issue isn't really the issue.

In a foundational way, it doesn't matter which issue is keeping someone outside the Church. There are myriad issues that drive or keep people away: sexual activity outside of marriage, support for abortion, lack of belief in the Real Presence of Jesus in the Eucharist. There can be issues for divorced and remarried couples, disagreement with a male priesthood, or agreement with cultural or political positions that run counter to Church teaching. American politics do not, after all, line up tidily with our faith. Part of our responsibility is to be educated in the fullness of Catholic teaching. We have to understand the issues ourselves before we can help others understand them.

What matters in the end is that through the process of conversion the Holy Spirit brings us face to face with the Catholic Church. Once we accept that the Church holds the truth, then we as pilgrims embark on an incredible journey that prompts us to examine every aspect of our lives in the light of God's truth. It's in that light that real change and ongoing conversion happen, no matter what issue brought us to that turning point.

If Our Lord respects the free will of his people, so must we. Our part is not to condemn the state of others' souls. We may certainly speak of the objective good or evil of an action, but we're called to remember that sins and sinners are not the same thing.

The goal, as Pope Benedict said, is to share the revelation that salvation is found in God's love. We must choose our words carefully and share them with a love like that of the Shepherd for his sheep.

My words can't force conversion on anyone, but my words do matter.

CHAPTER 9

Don't Forget How Hard It Is

I WAS BLINKING BACK TEARS, my eyes volleying from one RCIA team member to another.

"Well, certainly you *are* married," said one woman, "*legally* married."

"*Civilly* married," inserted a man.

"Civilly *and* legally married, because you were married by a judge," continued the first woman, nodding. "The Church *would* say you are married...."

"Well, *I* think I'm married," I said nervously (and possibly with hostility).

"Yes, the Church would say you are married," she repeated, nodding.

"I don't think so," one of the sponsors said, shaking her head. "I don't know about that."

"Well, you are *legally* married," said the first woman again, ignoring the sponsor.

"But spiritually ... " a second man threw in.

Spiritually what? I wondered. *You have no idea what shape my marriage is in, spiritually or otherwise.*

"Marriage," a third woman began enunciating carefully, "is, well ... " She looked as if she were about to say someone close to me had just died in a train wreck. "Marriage is a sacrament in the Catholic Church. And if you were married by a judge, well ... in a *Christian* marriage God gives gifts to the marriage that strengthen it and allow the two people to fulfill their vows." Her eyes darted uncomfortably around the room at the other team members as she shifted in her chair. "Your marriage might not be ... well ... you might have to ... ummm ..."

I gulped and looked around at the team. Some looked like deer caught in proverbial headlights. Others avoided my gaze. I couldn't believe what I was hearing, or perhaps more accurately what I wasn't hearing. What were they keeping from me? I couldn't become a Catholic? My marriage was a sham? *What were they saying?*

"We'll have to talk to Father, about all the particulars," one woman said, a worried crease still in her brow. "And we'll see what he says. Your husband might have to ... do something."

"Umm ... okay." I gulped. "Yeah. Well ... let me know. Because there is no way that my husband is going to do anything with the Catholic Church."

I was grateful when someone else asked another question and we shifted to a topic other than my clearly defective marriage. I was feeling dazed when, during a break, a kind, grandmotherly woman approached me and sat down next to me on the couch. "You know what?" she said, patting my hand. "I have a feeling. Your husband may be surprised one day. If you become a devout Catholic, he may eventually just follow you into the Church." She smiled. "So. Just don't you worry about a thing." She patted my hand again and looked sympathetically into my eyes.

"Thank you," I managed to croak, "but I don't know about that. I can't see him considering it." Tom had made that much clear to me. I wiped my eyes and excused myself. I appreciated her kindness, but after what I'd heard earlier I was worried.

As soon as the meeting was over, I dashed to my car and cried most of the way home. At the first RCIA meeting the previous week, I'd heard, "Oh, that's ... um, *different*," when I explained that I was inquiring on my own, that my husband wasn't Catholic. I was already tired, too, of hearing, "The family that prays together, stays together!" Tom and I would never pray together. I resented the implication. Still, I could set well-meaning platitudes aside, but the dissection of my marriage situation was too much. It was too hard.

*Why do these Catholics have to make **everything** so hard?* I thought.

Strange, Imaginary Fears

A few years before my baptism, I had a dream. I journaled:

> I was alone in a waiting room. Across the room, I saw a face on the cover of a magazine. I knew it was Jesus and that he was trying to reach me, but he never spoke. I was drawn and repelled at the same time. I couldn't move from the spot where I was sitting, even though I wanted to. I knew he had something to tell me, but I was too frightened to listen. I stared hard at that face, and even though there was something he wanted me to do—and I wanted to do it—I couldn't speak or move. I wanted to scream.

Trying to move from the darkness of unbelief into the light of belief can be paralyzing. Sometimes the dark seems more inviting. You *try*—you take a few tentative steps into an entirely new world. You have preconceived notions about "religious people," and "religious people" have preconceived notions about former atheists like you. Everything is new and incomprehensible. In church, you don't know when to sit, stand, kneel, or when to speak or say "Amen." You're learning, but you're still on the outside.

I know now that any judgments perceived or imagined weren't really important and really weren't about me. Ideally, I wouldn't have allowed such things to affect me so much. But if you've never been an outsider in a church community, try to imagine for a moment what it feels like. It's not easy being a pilgrim.

As a stranger in the strange land of RCIA, I attended Mass alone every Sunday. In the sea of people around me there was a common language, an exclusive club, a secret handshake. I was the misfit. Or at least it felt that way.

When I stayed in the pew while others went forward for holy Communion, I wondered if they were thinking, "What horrible sin did she commit that she can't receive?" It was awkward to have people step over me; I didn't know the etiquette. Should I get out of the pew, make room for them, and then sit back down? Or was I supposed to let them slide past me while I remained seated? I usually tried to take a seat on the end of a pew, but, inevitably, someone would scoot in next to me just as Mass was beginning, foiling my attempts to be both invisible and polite.

But greater than the etiquette confusion was my resentment at not being allowed to fully participate in the Mass. One week, I actually got up and left the church after the Liturgy of the Word. I know now I was being childish, practically stomping out, but at the time I felt hurt and annoyed that this institution could decide whether or not I was ready to receive the Eucharist. Who was this faceless bureaucracy that deemed itself capable of determining what was in my heart, that I did not believe "enough" to receive the Lord?

Before I even entered RCIA, I believed in the Real Presence of Jesus in the bread and wine. And I had now learned enough about Catholicism to understand about apostolic succession, holy orders, and validly ordained ministers of the sacraments. Ironically, now that I believed in the Catholic Church's power to bring me the true Eucharist—his real and healing Body and Blood, which I was aching to receive—I was denied access to him. I knew they wanted me to finish RCIA, but still. It was painful.

I complained to Jack about feeling like an outsider and not having a community. He said: "You do have one—it's the community of inquirers. For now, anyway." He suggested that I offer up my feelings of isolation and other sufferings and think of abstaining from the Eucharist not as a judgment pronounced on me but as a fast until I could be in complete agreement with the Church on all of the difficult issues. It made sense, but it wasn't easy.

When I read Thomas Merton's *Seven Storey Mountain*, I said: "Yes! *Yes!* He understands!" Despite all my self-consciousness, I wasn't crazy:

> Another thing which Catholics do not realize about converts is the tremendous, agonizing embarrassment and self-consciousness which they feel about praying publicly in a Catholic Church. The effort it takes to overcome all the strange imaginary fears that everyone is looking at you, and that they all think you are crazy or ridiculous, is something that costs a tremendous effort.[35]

Not only were there worries about what other Catholics were thinking of me, there were sometimes even conflicts with other converts. One night in RCIA class, I brought up a question. It was a rather technical one, as I'd recently had a long conversation with my brother-in-law, a Missouri Synod Lutheran pastor. I wanted to be able to meet his objections with accuracy regarding the Catholic viewpoint. I will never forget the exasperation in the voice of another candidate who said, "Do we really have to spend time on questions that are about as relevant to most of us as how many angels can dance on the head of a pin?" Some days I felt as if I couldn't win.

Practice Doesn't Always Make Perfect

If the RCIA process offers its own particular brand of unintentional intimidation, imagine a few steps back in time, to the evening when this self-conscious former atheist first walked alone into a Catholic church.

Though I'd gone to Mass with Jack in the past, Tom and I now lived a hundred miles away from Jack and Holly. I'd left the Episcopalians behind and was struggling to move on. I wanted to learn more about the Catholic Church, but to do so I was going to have to set foot in one.

We had moved to a tiny town where I didn't know any Catholics. If I were going to attend a Mass, I'd have to do it on my own. One day I took a deep breath, steeled myself, and called the church that was a few blocks from our home. An elderly priest answered the phone, and when I asked if he had a program for people who wanted to learn more about Catholicism ("My friend said they call it RCIA?") he laughed.

"It's been so long since anyone wanted one," he said. "I don't know … I guess if someone wanted something like that … well, I guess I could …" he trailed off.

"Um, okay, no," I said, feeling more shocked than rejected. I'd assumed priests were eager for new recruits and was stunned he would laugh off a serious inquirer. "Thank you anyway," I told him. "I think I'll just check into something else."

"If that's what you want," he said. I could almost hear his shrug.

"Um, yes, thanks. That's what I'll do."

Picking up the phone that day had been monumentally difficult, but the next phone call would be easier, right? Surely I wouldn't get turned down by two Catholic priests in one day.

I nervously called a larger church that was about thirty minutes from our home. The receptionist was polite and business-like as she listed the available Mass times. "Thank you very much!" I chirped, sounding, I hoped, like a veteran Catholic who called churches all the time. Mass at 5:30, Saturday evening. That could work.

Suddenly, though, I worried about every ridiculous detail I could conjure: What if I can't find the church? Where do I park? What door am I supposed to go in? Can you go in the side door of a church, or do you have to go through the front? Can I sit where

I won't be noticed? What if someone wants to talk to me, or asks me to join something? (I needn't have worried about that. These were Catholics.) I remembered telling Jack once: "There should be a service for beginners, like a training class. Then when training is over they could filter us into the main church. But maybe with you Catholics, there are no beginners."

Tom offered to assuage some of my panic by driving me to church and dropping me at the front door. He ran errands with our baby in tow while I headed into Mass. With sweaty palms and immense trepidation, I walked in, dipped my fingers in the holy water font, and crossed myself. *Okay, I look kind of Catholic so far, maybe no one will notice me.* I chose a pew near the back and sat down, my heart pounding.

The packed Mass was familiar from my days at Mass with Jack. Then came the awkward moment when everyone in the pew rose and went forward for holy Communion. I felt clumsy and conspicuous, as if a huge tattoo—*Sinner*—were inked on my forehead. *Oh, why did this have to be so hard?*

I certainly wasn't convinced I could be Catholic, but I *knew* I needed the Real Presence of Jesus Christ in the Eucharist. Could I actually be headed for Rome?

I wrote in my journal: "I can hear friends asking, 'Why Catholic?' I imagine them thinking, 'Why not something easier?' But I'm not looking for what's easy. I'm looking for what is true."

I took a bulletin home from that Mass. An announcement jumped out at me: "RCIA, Starting September 13th. If you are interested in joining us please call the rectory as soon as possible." Though every step of this journey made me shaky, I picked up the phone and signed myself up for RCIA.

That is how I ended up sitting on a couch, having my marriage dissected, and waiting to find out what shape the Catholic Church thought it was in.

I considered quitting, but decided to give it more time. The week after I drove home in tears, the newly ordained priest in charge of RCIA approached me before the meeting began. "I'm still not sure what to do about your case," he said.

Oh, no, I'm a case, I thought.

"I think you might have to take some classes," Fr. Ken continued, "along with your husband. And then if your husband decides to join the Church"—I hope I kept an eye roll in check here—"you can get your marriage blessed, but if he decides not to join, we can still get the marriage blessed, I *think, if* he will acknowledge and not be opposed to his responsibilities about your children."

I was speechless. Tom would agree to *nothing* about Catholicism. That was a fact. Was I doomed to remain a beggar at the gates? I sat through another meeting that night, barely caring what was discussed. All signs were pointing to the fact that none of it would apply to "my case."

When I told Jack about all of this, he picked up the phone, called the archdiocese, explained my marriage situation in detail, and was told that my marriage was valid. He also gave me the name of a Catholic apostolate that specialized in apologetics. I called them and was given the same answer Jack got. Hey! We had a real, live sacrament going on under our roof, and we didn't even know it.

It was three more weeks before Fr. Ken had an answer for me. He came into the RCIA meeting that night, beaming. "Your husband doesn't have to do a bloody thing!" he trumpeted. "Your marriage is valid! You are free to do whatever you want to do regarding your reception into the Church."

I hugged Fr. Ken, whom I was already coming to love, and withheld the fact that I'd already found an answer on my own. The important thing was I didn't have to drag Tom to meetings or convince him to give Catholicism a try. No more sticky Catholic red tape about my husband. All the tears and worries of the previous month had been wasted on a problem that didn't exist and that my friend had solved with one phone call.

A quick note of explanation about the circumstances of our marriage is in order: Tom was a baptized, lapsed Lutheran, and I was an unbaptized atheist when we got married, but because neither of us was Catholic we were not bound to the Catholic form of marriage. The Church recognizes the marriage of two non-Catholics as valid, no matter whether a judge or a pastor witnesses the marriage. And, in a shiny bonus round of information, I had been informed that at the moment of my baptism our marriage was supernaturally transformed into a sacramental marriage.

I didn't hold a grudge (well, not for very long) against team members who'd spoken about their concerns. They were good people doing their best, wrangling with the information I gave them. I didn't blame Fr. Ken either. He was new, overwhelmed, and stumbling his way through a million priestly duties every day. I learned that in marriage law, while some cases are straightforward, there are so many nuances and variables that attempting to navigate it can be like tiptoeing through a minefield in clown shoes. Some areas of Church law are best left to the canon lawyers and resident experts, and marriage is one of those areas.

Jack's wife, Holly, had gone through an emotional roller coaster regarding the state of her marriage, too. "We had to have our marriage blessed," Holly told me, "since we'd been married in the Presbyterian Church. I was bothered by that because it seemed like they weren't acknowledging that we were married. One of the members of our prayer group expressed disappointment that they hadn't been invited to be there when our marriage was blessed, but we did it very privately just to get over that hurdle to join the Church."

Even though Holly had freely chosen to join the Church, it was still hard to make her Catholic friends understand that what they saw as a joyous occasion and the fulfillment of her marriage status, she saw as a sensitive, hurtful sticking point. She didn't deny the necessity of the action, she just wished her friends could understand why it was difficult for her.

When I talked to Jack about the spectrum of my reactions—from hostility, fear, and tears, to patiently awaiting a reply, to amusement about the fact that he'd gotten the correct answer with a quick phone call—he reminded me that although the Church is divinely guided in matters of faith and morals, the earthly Church is an imperfect institution that houses a necessary bureaucracy full of requisite records, details, and fact checks.

"I get it," I told him. On an intellectual level, the Church did not have to defend its fact-checking and inquiry processes to me. Practically speaking, I knew that kind of stuff was unavoidable.

"I understand all that," I told Jack. "I even agree with it."

"You agree with it in *theory*," he said.

"In theory *and* in practice," I conceded. "But the fact that I *agree* doesn't make the *practice* of this theory any easier. It's *hard*. And it's not perfect."

"I know," agreed the man whose wife had also found the technicalities of conversion irksome, "it's not perfect. But it's the only thing we've got."

In All Things Charity

Since becoming a Catholic twenty years ago, I've learned a lot more about the perfection and imperfection of the Catholic Church, about what's hard in Catholicism and what doesn't have to be.

There's plenty about converting to Catholicism that *is* hard. Giving up your identity and letting God turn your world upside down is hard. Opening yourself up to a new community is hard. Being the only Catholic in your family is hard. Learning what Catholic doctrine is, what's nonnegotiable, and then promising to live differently is hard. Conversion, as Thomas Merton said, involves things that cost "a tremendous effort."

But the hard edges of conversion can be softened with kindness and understanding from those already in the fold. Even a brief acknowledgment that the steps of conversion are difficult helps the pilgrim along his path. And once he's in the fold, we don't want to make things harder than they need to be. Unnecessary division can be a source of scandal. There will always be camps within Catholicism as there will be in any diverse group of human beings, but the Church allows for a wide expression of spirituality, and as long as we agree on doctrinal issues there's room for varying opinions in areas of choice. "Have nothing to do with stupid, senseless controversies," we read in the Second Letter of Timothy, "you know that they breed quarrels" (2:23).

In a way, I was right way back when I thought Catholicism was like a club—the best and most welcoming aspects of a club. It *is* a community in which we all share the best thing in the world— new life in Jesus Christ. There's no secret handshake and no uncharitable exclusion, but there are periodic misunderstandings that inadvertently makes things tougher on newcomers. The old adage, "In essentials, unity, in nonessentials, liberty, in all things, charity," should be the motto of Camp Catholic, where we gather at the end of the day to support one another and tell our stories. Because whatever we can do within the boundaries of magisterial teaching to make it easier for others to join, we should do enthusiastically.

"All things are possible with God, but all things are not easy."

—George MacDonald[36]

CHAPTER 10

Don't Limit the Definition of a Personal Relationship

"Being Christian is not the result of an ethical
choice or a lofty idea, but the encounter with an
event, a person, which gives life a new horizon
and a decisive direction."

—Pope Benedict XVI[37]

IN WHICH "PERSONAL RELATIONSHIP WITH JESUS" camp do you
pitch your tent? When you hear someone say, "Genuine faith is
about a personal relationship with Jesus Christ," do you scoff at a
trendy presumption or do the words strike a chord?

If you're in Camp A and find yourself scoffing, perhaps you're
concerned about the terminology or worry that such vocabulary
invites subjectivism where it doesn't belong: "Jesus is supposed to
be my pal? It's not about how I *feel* that matters—feelings change.
It's about being faithful. I go to confession, I go to Mass, and I receive holy Communion every week. It doesn't—and doesn't need
to—get more personal than that."

Perhaps you fall into Camp B and the words "personal relationship" not only strike a chord, they make you want to strike
up the band. You enthusiastically agree: "Exactly! If I don't have a

relationship with Jesus Christ, what's the point? My faith would be dry and meaningless."

It's true that we Catholics are as cozy with God as it gets, thanks to holy Communion. It really *doesn't* get more intimate than consuming the Body, Blood, Soul, and Divinity of Jesus Christ in the Eucharist. On the other hand, the Lord also invites us to cultivate a growing, ongoing relationship with him outside of Sunday Mass. If we ignore that, we miss many of the riches God has to offer us.

But discussing personal relationships gets, well, *personal*. So, before we get started, let's set some boundaries: No one in Camp A will be pushed to hug a stranger while singing "Kumbaya" and no one in Camp B will be forced into an empty, pharisaical practice of faith. Are we ready?

Let's put aside preconceived notions of what a personal relationship with Jesus is or what we think it should be and take a closer look at what the concept really means. We might be surprised to find there's no need for separate camps, that there's a sane and balanced road to walk. This is not an either/or situation. We humans are complex beings, and the truth of our relationship with Jesus Christ deserves more than sound bites on social media.

A Tale of Two Catholics

Karl—we've already encountered him in his wife Danae's story— grew up in nondenominational, evangelical churches. From the time he was very young, his parents encouraged him to give his life to Jesus in a personal and meaningful way. They taught him to seek God's will for his life through prayer and Scripture reading, and they modeled a loving, active faith. They immersed their son in communities made up of passionate Christians.

It worked. Karl loved Jesus Christ. But there was a sticking point for him. Even as a teen, Karl, with his introspective, contemplative personality, preferred quiet study and reflection as his worship companions over the contemporary Christian rock that was the norm in his church. A talented singer and musician himself, Karl thought the music of his church didn't reach far enough or dig deep enough to convey the profundity of the teachings of Christ. Rather than stirring his passion for God, the worship style Karl grew up with left him cold.

In high school and college Karl had marvelous travel opportunities and he attended some Eastern-rite liturgies. It was like visiting a new planet. "I felt as though the prayers and the ritual opened up my soul to receive a flood of graces and love," he said. "Here was worship steeped in history, transmitted from saint to saint throughout the generations, reaching back to Jesus Christ and Judaism. This was the most profound worship experience I had ever had."

Karl's upbringing had already taught him that faith was more than going through the motions of church attendance. He already had precisely what his church had always stressed—a personal relationship with Jesus Christ. He prayed, he sought God's will in everything he did, and he loved the Lord. But it was in discovering the depth and beauty of ritual and liturgy that his soul was set on fire. A flame was kindled and, although he didn't yet know it, Karl was primed to make his way into the Catholic Church.

After college, Karl pursued work as a church music director. He was working at a Presbyterian church and attending Sunday worship there—his *modus operandi* was to worship at whichever church currently employed him. Then he met Danae, a Catholic who knew her faith inside and out. When Karl and Danae embarked on a serious relationship, they talked about their respective religious practices. Danae's ability to answer questions about her convictions impressed Karl. He found himself yearning for what she had: a spiritual home and compelling reasons for living there.

They got engaged. Karl had a number of questions, so he did what he'd done growing up: he sought God's will through prayer. One thing he repeatedly returned to was how powerfully he felt

God's presence in liturgy and ritual. Shortly before his wedding, Karl made a decision: he wanted to be received into the Catholic Church.

Solemn, reverent worship had been a powerful tool in his own conversion, and Karl has seen it have a similar effect on others. As the liturgy and music director at a large, Midwestern Catholic parish, Karl brings beauty to the Mass every Sunday morning. He knows that beauty is one of the most powerful witnesses for Christ we can share, and he shares it every week with hundreds of people. His personal relationship with Christ is alive and well.

Kevin's story is different. Kevin grew up Catholic. He left the faith for a time, but studied his way back into the church of his childhood. He became a strong, well-catechized Catholic, passionately in love with Jesus. Married, a father of four, and a home-schooling dad, Kevin and his wife, Kelly, wanted to share the faith with their children as fully as they could.

Their parish and its vibrant priest initially seemed perfect for them. Over the course of a couple of years, their pastor made some changes at the parish. He reinstituted sung Masses, added chant, introduced Mass parts in Latin, and brought back the Communion rail. The church itself was a beautiful and majestic place, and the Mass was beautiful and solemn, too.

Yet for Kevin and Kelly, something seemed to be missing. While many of their friends thought the pastor's changes rendered the Mass more beautiful, Kevin and Kelly had lost something. They migrated to a parish that offered a reverent but somewhat more modern style, one in which they were more comfortable. Their new parish rekindled the flame they'd felt flickering; they felt at home again.

Both Karl and Kevin attend churches that are faithful to the magisterium of the Catholic Church. Both worship at valid, licit Masses with music approved by their bishops. And each of them has a personal relationship with Jesus Christ.

Obviously, the depth and quality of a relationship with the Lord cannot be reduced to or defined by musical or liturgical styles and preferences. But if we treat music as a metaphor for the textures and flavors of relationship, we see there's a rich variety of ways in which to have a "personal relationship with Jesus Christ."

That Thing Like a Love Affair

A common reaction against the assertion that we need a personal relationship with Jesus is that it's unnecessary if we are regularly and frequently partaking of the sacraments of the Catholic Church. Let's examine that. First of all, what is a sacrament? A sacrament is an outward sign of an inward grace. The seven sacraments were instituted by Christ, and he gave us these gifts as a means of drawing us closer to him and effecting our ongoing sanctification. By definition, receiving a sacrament—receiving Christ's gift—is already personal. So it's true that in receiving sacraments we are already engaging in a personal relationship with Christ. Does it stop there?

The Catechism of the Catholic Church tells us, "The Eucharist is the source and summit of the Christian life," and that "the other sacraments, and indeed all ecclesiastical ministries and works of the apostolate, are bound up with the Eucharist and are oriented toward it. For in the blessed Eucharist is contained the whole spiritual good of the Church, namely Christ himself, our Pasch" (1324).

And further, as Pope Benedict XVI put it:

We are only Christians if we encounter Christ. Of course, he does not show himself to us in this overwhelming, luminous way, as he did to Paul to make him the Apostle to all peoples. But we too can encounter Christ in reading sacred Scripture, in prayer, in the liturgical life of the Church. We can touch Christ's heart and feel him touching ours. Only in this personal relationship with Christ, only in this encounter with the Risen One do we truly become Christians.[38]

A relationship with God, as we saw in chapter two, is akin to a marriage. I would be appalled if Tom said to me, "Hey, we went through that ceremony, we're legally bound, and we meet up regularly for sex, which is as intimate as it gets. Why do you need more?" Clearly some vital aspects of "relationship" would be missing: affection, attention, respect, partnership, and conversation, just for starters.

In our marriage, I trust Tom with my feelings, sufferings, and joys. Our relationship has richness, depth, and honesty. My husband isn't a casual friend to whom I toss an occasional hello or meet for a monthly coffee date. If either of us tried to treat it that way, we'd have more than a little problem.

My relationship with the Lord cries out for the same care. It demands much more than showing up once a week for the main event, that most intimate union, the Eucharist. It demands what a marriage calls for: diligent attention, complete self-donation, and the reception of whatever God wants to give me in return.

A Personal, Intimate Encounter

The idea of a personal relationship with Jesus is a concept that is as old as creation. In the Book of Deuteronomy we are told we are to "love the Lord your God with all your heart, and with all your soul, and with all your might" (6:5). This command is repeated throughout the New Testament (see Mt 22:37; Mk 12:30,33; and Lk 10:27). In the prologue of the Catechism of the Catholic Church we're told, "At every time and in every place, God draws close" to us. He calls us "to seek him, to know him, to love him with all [our] strength" (1). This "intimate and vital bond" of humanity with God is at the heart of our faith (see 29). Pope Benedict, too, spoke of this bond when he said:

> And this, dear brothers and sisters, is true for every Christian: Faith is above all a personal, intimate encounter with Jesus, and to experience his closeness, his friendship, his love; only in this way does one learn to know him ever more, and to love and follow him ever more. May this happen to each one of us.[39]

What does this bond and encounter look like? My friend Jen, who told me that her mother has always spoken to Jesus as if he is her best friend, is grateful for the example of personal relationship she grew up with. Her mother helps her see that trust is at the core of her relationship with the Lord. "I have a tendency to over think things," said Jen, "to worry, and seek to control so that I can feel less lost, especially when life isn't easy. My mom's faith has encouraged me to trust in Jesus, especially when I'm worrying or afraid."

My friend Holly, speaking again of her dear friend Pat—the woman who became godmother to their family—said that Pat modeled a personal relationship with the Lord for her. "Pat started a youth group," Holly said, "but before we actually met with the teens, she asked those of us she'd recruited as leaders to pray together in her home for several months. We shared our lives and prayed with Scripture." This small group experience was transformational for Holly.

She added that in looking back there were other friends who became role models for her. The personal relationships she observed all looked different from the outside, and some seemed very simple, but what they shared was deep, internal devotion to Christ. "Looking back on my childhood," Holly said, "my best friend was Catholic, and I remember their family not eating meat on Fridays. I remember the crucifixes in their house. Later, with Jack at Mass, I looked at the old women who arrived at church before I got there,

praying their rosaries in the front pew. All of these practices of the
Faith made it seem so steadfast to me." That steadfastness is what
St. John Paul II referred to when he said:

> [Conversion] gives rise to a dynamic and lifelong pro-
> cess which demands a continual turning away from 'life
> according to the flesh' to 'life according to the Spirit' (cf.
> Rom 8:3-13). Conversion means accepting, by a personal
> decision, the saving sovereignty of Christ and becoming
> his disciple.[40]

A relationship with Jesus Christ sometimes begins with intellectual assent. For me, and for many converts like me, certain intellectual concerns have to be addressed before we can even begin
to consider the faith. But it cannot stop there. "Intellectual assent is
but one aspect of an integrated life of faith," says Dr. Carole Brown.
"By definition, a sacrament is something that causes what it signi-
fies. If the Church is a 'sacrament of intimate union with God,'
then it follows that such an intimate union is not only possible
for baptized believers, but a normative description of what mature
faith is."[41]

Mature faith, like mature friendship, love, and marriage, is
layered, complex, and yearns for depth of expression. It is never
merely external or superficial in character. But just as human relationships vary in what they look like, so will our relationships with
the Divine. A personal relationship won't look exactly the same in
everyone. We can't limit a personal relationship with the Lord to
being either "all about feelings" or "only" receiving the sacraments.
It's both/and, not either/or.

Catholicism, as its name implies, is a universal faith. We will
always find variances in the ways the Faith is lived and expressed.
Witness the many forms of spirituality, from Benedictine to Do-
minican, to Franciscan and so many others. The Church approves

all of them. A personal relationship with Jesus Christ is not about choosing a camp. It's about, as Pope Francis said:

> Our own constantly renewed experience of savoring Christ's friendship and his message. It is impossible to persevere in a fervent evangelization unless we are convinced from personal experience that it is not the same thing to have known Jesus, as not to have known him, not the same thing to walk with him, as to walk blindly, not the same thing to hear his word, as not to know it, and not the same thing to contemplate him, to worship him, to find our peace in him, as not to.[42]

Scripture, the Catechism, popes, the Fathers of the Church, and other saints have taught us that a relationship with the Person of Jesus is at the core of our faith. More accurately, that relationship *is* our faith. To be a Christian is to have, and to seek a deeper, relationship with Jesus Christ. We needn't get bogged down in language or labels, "shoulds" and "shouldn'ts" about what a relationship looks like. And since we can't see into the heart of another, we needn't opine on whether or not they're doing it right.

From the charismatic college student to the little old lady steadfastly praying the Rosary to the hipster who loves chant, personal relationships are, well, personal. Every story I've shared in these pages is the story of a personal relationship with the Lord. The variety of those stories is powerful proof that God manifests his friendship and spreads his Word in a kaleidoscope of ways.

There's no single definition of a personal relationship, and there is nothing un-Catholic about pursuing that intimate bond. Just be yourself. Be personal. Encounter Christ.

> "Do not wish to be anything but what you are, and try to be that perfectly."
>
>   —St. Francis de Sales[43]

CHAPTER 11

Don't Assume You Are Speaking the Same Language

"There are not over a hundred people in the
United States who hate the Catholic Church.
There are millions, however, who hate what they
wrongly believe to be the Catholic Church—
which is, of course, quite a different thing."
—Archbishop Fulton Sheen

ARCHBISHOP SHEEN'S FREQUENTLY CITED COMMENT has survived for the very good reason that it's true. Millions of people grow up with misconceptions, stereotypes, misguided notions, and downright wonky ideas about what the Catholic Church is. Evangelization is sometimes as subtle as gently correcting a mistaken notion, offering a friend a previously overlooked puzzle piece, or clarifying a word choice.

I remember my early interrogations of my Christian friends about their faith. I was out for dinner one night with a group, some of whom were Catholic, some nondenominational Protestants, all passionate, and, once I started asking, all ready to talk. As we polished off the last of the fries, refilled our coffee, and ordered pie, I was struck by the fact that an enormous amount of translating had been going on all evening. We weren't speaking the same language.

"Sad Simplification"

Jack had known for some time that I lacked a particular type of knowledge. It wasn't just my ignorance of history and doctrinal issues. I lacked fluency in the general language of religion, as well as the denominational vernacular of Christianity. Jack always began conversations with caveats about Catholic peculiarities and stopped to define terms as we talked. I took it all in like an eager student learning a foreign language. Religion *was* a foreign language. A "simple" conversation with a Catholic was never simple to me.

The night I was out with my ecumenical group of friends, I said something about growing up without religion. Zac, who had been raised in a Baptist denomination said: "Look, Karen, you can't be an American and *not* know what Christianity is. You're surrounded by it. It's everywhere. You can't deny that you grew up with religion. We all did. And since you grew up with it, you have a responsibility to respond to it, one way or another. You can either accept or reject it. That's totally up to you, but you *can't* say you haven't been presented with the Gospel."

I was taken aback. Did we live in different galaxies? I had not grown up with Christianity, not in the way Zac implied. It was true that I knew Christianity existed; I also knew that China existed, but I had never experienced China personally in a real or meaningful way. To say that I grew up with Christianity just because we did Santa Claus seemed as absurd as saying I understood Chinese culture because I've eaten fried rice with chopsticks.

"Not only *can* I say that I grew up without religion," I told Zac, "I *do* say that." I tried to explain what I meant.

"Here's what it was like. I grew up outside of Christianity. We didn't go to church, we didn't have relatives who went to church, and I didn't ask any of my churchgoing friends (well, at least not back then) to tell me about their god. It just wasn't an issue. What

I knew of Christianity was this: There are a lot of people who call themselves Christians, but they don't seem to look or act differently from anyone else, including my family."

Zac listened attentively.

"Beyond that," I continued, "I can't say I thought much about it. For a long time I operated under the mistaken assumption that we were some sort of generic Christian family, just because we celebrated Christmas and Easter. But I didn't really have any idea what those holidays meant beyond a rudimentary understanding that I'd gained from holiday specials. Yes, I knew that Christmas celebrated the birth of Jesus and Easter was about him rising from the dead. But *why* was he born into this world, *why* was he crucified, *why* did he rise from the dead? And how could any of it possibly affect or help me? I had no idea. I just unwrapped the Christmas presents and ate the chocolate eggs."

Zac laughed, and I went on.

"When I did think about Christianity it sounded ridiculous and impossible. A virgin got pregnant and gave birth to a god who somehow became a man? A big, shiny star and some kings? It sounded like a myth. And how does one man's suffering and death change anything about my *own* life and death? What could it mean that someone else 'died for my sins'? So, yes, I was exposed to the trappings of Christianity, but I was no more steeped in it than I was steeped in Hinduism because I'd seen *Ghandi*. Just because I grew up hearing Linus van Pelt tell me, 'That's what Christmas is all about, Charlie Brown,' doesn't mean I knew what Christmas was all about. You think I've rejected God, but I don't know if I know enough about him to reject him."

Zac admitted that he'd never thought of it that way. He'd been approaching me as if I were an apostate when in reality I had simply been an ignorant outsider.

By this time, though, I'd been learning more about Christianity. It still seemed quite improbable to me. I didn't enumerate all my objections that night, but among my qualms were things I'd later learn were defined as scandal—public, visible stumbling blocks, such as televangelists who preached poverty while living lives of excess, or politicians who spouted family values but were exposed as duplicitous liars left me shaking my head. *That's the religion they want me to follow?* I thought. (The priest-abuse scandal that would later shake me and ignite new questions had not yet come to light.)

On top of public, dubious examples of Christian behavior, I had doubts about the intellectual heft of the religion. Though I admit now that my presumptions were based on misunderstanding, at the time I thought I had a firm grasp on what "all of Christianity" taught. I would later discover that many of my objections to Christianity were, in fact, objections to ideas that were modern or fundamentalist departures from Catholic doctrine. When I learned the Catholic positions on issues, they made alarmingly good sense. But initially, based on the generally awful press Christianity got, I dismissed religion as hypocritical, simplistic, anti-intellectual, and anti-science.

Zac and Jack had a lot of walls to break down. I must admit now, though, that G. K. Chesterton had my number when he said that an atheist is often someone "limited and constrained by his own logic to a very sad simplification."[44]

It took the patience of Job for my friends to walk me through a period of extended examination of my sad simplifications, but they did me a very big favor from the start. They invited me into their circle, and they let me be myself. And when I was ready to ask, they let me start at the beginning, asking foundational, basic questions. I was an eager student who had signed up for Christianity 101, and my friends were my kindly professors. Little by little they helped to shape my perception of what Christianity is really all about.

Vocabulary Test

Christianity has a vocabulary all its own:

> Atonement, expiation, elect, redemption, repentance, revelation, justification, eschatology, apostle, apocalypse, Trinity, original sin, Messiah, resurrection, Pentecost, evangelical, synoptic Gospels.

Sheesh, get me a dictionary.

Catholicism gets even worse:

> Holy Sacrifice of the Mass, Eucharist, indulgence, novena, sacred Tradition (*Don't forget the difference between sacred Tradition and small t tradition!*), Blessed Mother, Our Lady, Hail Mary, Communion of Saints, Advent, Lent, liturgical year, Stations of the Cross, apostolate, Sunday obligation, Paschal Mystery, infallible, transubstantiation, chrism, catechesis, reconciliation.

Sheesh, take me to your leader.

Listening to Jack talk was always exasperating, humbling, or both. Sometimes I thought I knew what he was talking about only to find out that, once again, I was being a moron. There we'd be, sitting in Perkins, drinking coffee, and I'd say something like: "Well, some of this stuff about Mary makes sense, but I just can't believe in that Immaculate Conception thing. How am I supposed to believe that Jesus was conceived without sex being involved? What's wrong with sex?"

At this point, Jack would either sigh, or widen his eyes and swallow some coffee as he tried to formulate a kind, courteous response to my most recent ridiculous, naive, or grossly inaccurate assertion. "Well, you see, 'Immaculate Conception' doesn't refer to the virgin birth at all," he'd explain politely. "We call the virgin birth *the virgin birth*. Umm, I'll get to that in a minute. But the Immaculate Conception refers to the fact that Mary was born without the stain of original sin. It doesn't have anything to do with the conception of Jesus. It's about *Mary*, it's about God effecting her salvation at the moment she was conceived."

Then I'd say something cutting and intelligent like, "Oh." Jack would nod and explain the Immaculate Conception in more detail, and I'd be able to tick another issue off my list. It happened again and again. Infallible? Explain, please. *Ex Cathedra?* Jack, please go into Catholic-Merriam Webster mode. It was humbling to learn that I had been *so wrong for years about things I'd thought I understood.*

We had countless discussions over coffee about doctrines that I misunderstood, misinterpreted, had never heard of, or had trouble accepting: the male priesthood, purgatory, the assumption of Mary, confession, birth control, the pope. Questions led to new questions: Why Ash Wednesday? What's the point of Lent? When were Joseph and Mary married? Why is God so vindictive in the Old Testament? Why are you Catholics so stingy about Communion? What's with the rosary? Why is Mass an obligation? If you love God, don't you want to go to Mass? Why all this stuff about obedience and surrender? Isn't Christianity just another way to subjugate women?

At this point, Jack might have suggested that I switch to decaf.

Whether we're talking with non-Catholics, fallen-away Catholics, practicing Catholics, people of other religions, agnostics, or atheists, we simply can't assume we are speaking the same language. When I was an atheist, I made arguments against Christianity based on sweeping generalizations gathered from secular media or fundamentalist strains of Christian faith. Only after Jack defined a term for me in the language of Catholicism were we able to move on. Even faithful, practicing Catholics have wildly varying degrees of catechesis. As we look for common ground and a common language, remember to be patient. There's always another coffee date around the corner.

Another Kind of Language

In the midst of my spiritual trek, Tom took us on another trek. His job moved us five hundred miles away, but Jack and Zac didn't stop teaching me the language of Christianity. They never seemed to tire of my questions, and they let me in on a secret: even though Jesus was part of their native language, I wasn't always alone in my confusion. I loved Zac's honesty. He wrote me long letters detailing how he, too, sometimes felt confused by the various Christian denominations. Even though he'd found a church he was comfortable with, he disliked the structure and organization of religion, and deplored the divisions.

Jack talked to me about the vocabulary of prayer: dry prayer, heartfelt prayer, contemplative prayer, no prayer, prayers that went unanswered, prayer that lifted one to the heights of belief and joy. I didn't feel qualified to pray (as if it required a professional certificate of some kind), but both of my dear friends assured me that talking to God didn't have to wait until I considered myself a Christian.

So I started to pray, as meager and imperfect as I felt my attempts were. I prayed before I knew exactly who or what I was praying to, but it seemed as if it would be worth a try. Jack had given me a Catholic Bible, and I found the Our Father in its pages. I decided to pray it every day, spending minutes at a time on each word or phrase:

Our Father: (*What does it mean that he is my father? How does he provide for me? What does it mean that I am his daughter? If he is OUR father, what does that say about my relationship with others who call him father?*)

I did this for months, not realizing that I was practicing *Lectio Divina* ("Divine Reading"), a way of reading and praying with Scripture, slowly contemplating God's word and receiving it into your heart.

In an earlier chapter, I mentioned that some things are fatal to atheism. Reading the Bible and praying top the list. I had opened a door. Soon Jesus would poke his head in and ask: "Do you want me to come in now? It's up to you, really."

I awoke one day, weeping, with the words, "Jesus Christ, my Lord, my Savior, have mercy on my soul," on my lips and in my heart. I knew something in my gut: I believed. The ground beneath me had shifted and everything looked a little different. I was a believer, but I was a believer who was still a little afraid of believing.

I wondered, do I start calling myself a Christian now? I shunned the label, but not because of the arrogance I had once felt. No, I now knew that I couldn't call myself a Christian because I wasn't worthy of the name. At one time I'd considered myself "above Christianity," but now I grasped something that all faithful Christians know: Jesus Christ is so unfathomably above me that I can't even comprehend his boundless love. I didn't deserve him, but somehow he came to me anyway. It was—unbelievable, happy day!—a thing like a love affair.

My two best and sensible Christian friends told me I'd be foolish to wait until I considered myself "good enough" to call myself a Christian. "There was only one perfect Christian," Zac told me, "and he died on the cross for us." ("Well, Zac's right, in a way," Jack would add later, "but let's also talk a little more about Mary, conceived without sin ... ")

I would *never* be good enough to adopt the Christian label. At the same time, because Jesus loves me, I possess everything I need. I was experiencing the paradoxical astonishment that St. John Paul II spoke of in *Redeemer of Man*:

How precious must man be in the eyes of the Creator, if he "gained so great a Redeemer," and if God "gave his only Son" in order that man "should not perish but have eternal life." In reality, the name for that deep amazement at man's worth and dignity is the Gospel, that is to say: the Good News. It is also called Christianity. (10)

I was still a stranger in a strange land and still had a great deal of studying to do. But I finally spoke the language of faith well enough to articulate at least this: I was a believer. I was a lover of Christ.

Now that I have been a Catholic for twenty years, I speak the language so fluently that I sometimes forget those days when it was so hard to decipher words and concepts that were as foreign as hieroglyphics. I try to hang on to those memories, though, to remember what it felt like to land in a foreign country and grapple with a culture I couldn't comprehend. For those who don't yet know the lingo, I pray I can be the kind of guide that my friends were to me. Instead of dismissing me as one who rejected the Gospel, they spoke the words of the Gospel to me. And in translating the Good News to my unaccustomed ears, they transmitted God's love to me.

CHAPTER 12

Don't Pretend the Pilgrim Church Is Perfect

WHETHER JAMES JOYCE ACTUALLY SAID IT OR NOT, "Here comes everybody" aptly describes the Catholic Church.

In my parish of more than two thousand families, a holy day of obligation is a packed affair, celebrated with a bilingual Mass to accommodate a diverse population. That means I don't understand half of what is said because my Spanish is woefully lacking. Sometimes all the songs are in Spanish, too, but I love that because it reminds of the universal nature of the church. When the homily is delivered in English and Spanish, requiring patience from the entire assembly, I'm humbled. Such patience calls us to care for and about each other as fellow members of fallen humanity.

Here comes everybody.

Sometimes on Ash Wednesday I feel especially fallen. Ashes on my forehead, bits of ash flaking, falling on my nose. Smudged ash on my hands after I bury my face in prayer. I'm disheveled, distracted, hungry, in need of redemption.

Working class, blue collar, the wealthy, and affluent. Teachers, plumbers, writers, waitresses. Attorneys, contractors, tellers, mechanics. Web designers, students, poets. Dog lovers, cat ladies, animal haters, hamster people. Jeans, suits, ties, dresses, pants, skirts, little girls in glitter. The elderly and middle-aged. Gurgling babies, shrieking babies, sleeping babies. Sleepy mommies, widows, dads, college women, high school boys. Sad, lonely, beaming, concerned, frustrated, contented faces. Holy Mass. Confession lines. Kneeling in adoration. Here comes everybody.

My faith is imperfect and shifting: a mountaintop high, an ocean-depth low. It is the core of my being but sometimes the source of my frustration. It is beautiful and hard, strengthening and challenging. Faith is at every moment in my bones but sometimes so far from my heart I want to cry. Faith is, as C. S. Lewis said, "the art of holding on to things your reason has once accepted." Faith is mystery.

Mystery cries out to be addressed, in one way or another. Some time after my conversion, I thought about Henry David Thoreau and his explanation of why he took to the woods:

> I went to the woods because I wished to live deliberately, to front only the essential facts of life, and see if I could not learn what it had to teach, and not, when I came to die, discover that I had not lived.[45]

I lived for a long time without knowing why I was living. Now that I have claimed Christ as my core, I want what Thoreau sought: a deliberate life. I want to live with conviction, love, and purpose, the knowledge of who I am and what I believe. Since becoming a Catholic, my life is still unquestionably full of twists and turns, alarming developments, chaotic days, and sometimes anguished nights, but I can say with certainty: I know who I am. I live deliberately and with mystery.

I have reframed Thoreau's words to illuminate my own path:

> I followed Jesus Christ because I wished to live deliberately, to front only the essential facts of life, and see if I could not learn what Jesus had to teach, and not, when I came to die, discover that I had not truly lived for and loved him.

After such a search, after so much reflection, years of pain, uncomfortable family relationships, and misunderstandings with people who couldn't imagine why I'd want to become Catholic, obviously I can also say with certainty that the reason it was all worth it is that the Catholic Church, the institution Jesus handed over to the keeping of the Holy Spirit, is perfect.

Right?

Perhaps not. But it is the perfect place to be, and the perfect place to live in mystery.

Be It Ever So Little

G. K. Chesterton once said that the only unanswerable argument against Christianity was Christians, that we "prove conclusively what the Bible teaches about the Fall."[46]

Scripture's parable of the wheat and the tares reminds us that the Church is both human and divine. Because Jesus gave us the Church, we can be sure it is a divine institution: created, guided, and sustained by the Lord. At the same time, the earthly organizational chart reveals a collection of flawed souls.

When I first started attending various churches as an inquirer, I remember feeling alienated sometimes by "proper" religious people. I felt sized up, judged, found wanting or too worldly. Whether it stemmed from the way I dressed, or my ignorance of Christianity, or my incessant questions and challenges, I sometimes felt that instead of being invited to meet the most wondrous Person in the world—the Someone who would change my life—I was being sized up for membership in a social club.

Denominational infighting scandalized me. Later on, warring camps within Catholicism scandalized me, too. *Why is the Body of Christ so broken?* I wondered. The *Catechism* addresses many of the reasons people might reject God. "The scandal of bad example on the part of believers" (29) is certainly one of those reasons. We *all* fail in the day-to-day execution of Christian charity. After joining the Church, I know I, too, have been too rigid, have judged, have failed to transmit the love of God.

Worse than everyday lapses of Christian charity, though, are the horrific offenses. The priest-abuse scandal that rocked the Catholic Church in recent years was unspeakably ugly. The pain, suffering, and betrayal caused by abusers who traded on their trust and power, and the denial and coverups of some Church leaders provoked the righteous anger of millions, including Tom and me. *Why is the Body of Christ so broken?* There is no excuse, no justification, no apologetic attempt that explains or rationalizes away what happened. There is only sin in a fallen world. Where free will exists, evil choices will be made, by those within and outside the Church. Cold comfort, that.

"But shouldn't the Church be *different*?" we ask. "Shouldn't the Church be held to a higher standard? Oughtn't we to expect more of those who are following Christ?"

Yes. It *should* be different. There *is* a higher standard. We *do* expect more. Jesus *wants* those of us in the pilgrim Church to tirelessly strive for holiness. But there's a catch: "The Church" starts with me.

"He does much," said St. Peter of Alcantara, "in the sight of God who does his best, be it ever so little."[47]

That littleness is the daily call of my deliberate life.

Putting Up with Ourselves

"I saw about a peck of counterfeit dollars once," American Presbyterian evangelist William Biederwolf purportedly said. "Did I go to the window and throw away all my good dollars? No! Yet you reject Christianity because there are hypocrites, or counterfeit Christians."

I kept a tight grip on "the hypocrisy argument" for a long time when I was an atheist. "If Christianity is true," I thought, "wouldn't Christians be better at it? Shouldn't you guys have changed the world by now?" I remember telling Jack that I couldn't possibly become a Christian. "Why would I want to?" I asked. "When I look around a church, any church, all I see is a bunch of hypocrites." Jack shot back: "Well, come on in and join us. There's always room for one more."

Zing. When challenged to face my own imperfections and countless faults, I suddenly saw the pilgrim Church in a new light. The Church, I realized, was made up of people just like me—messy, struggling blunderers, but blunderers who are *trying*. Wounded souls who want sanctity, despite the fact that they still regularly trip over it. Once I grasped this, "organized religion" made sense. We *need* each other. We have to band together to do better.

I eventually tried to help flip the same switch for Tom. One day, when he was finally beginning to believe that Jesus is God, Tom told me I'd helped him rethink religion. He admitted that over the years he'd crafted and held on to a prejudice against religion because of all the evil done in its name. He said I had pointed out to him that the existence of hypocrisy didn't negate the existence of objective truth. Rather, the very fact that we perceive hypocrisy points to an ideal that we believe in and against which we measure everything else. The trick is in recognizing that I am part of "everything else."

Rejecting Christianity because its ranks were made up of fallen humans was like saying I wouldn't enter a crowded restaurant because it was full of hungry people. My excuses were really just another way to dodge commitment. It was easier to be dismissive, judgmental, and condescending to Christians than to engage with them. What I learned was that authentic, robust Christianity does indeed challenge us to face up to our own hypocrisy. There are strong passages in Scripture about failure to live up to the demands of faith. For starters, see Jesus' chilling repetition of woes—"woe to you, hypocrites"—as he berates the scribes and Pharisees who "preach and do not practice" (Mt 23:1-36).

Jesus did not complacently tolerate pharisaical hypocrisy. His intentions were clear when it came to those who persist in known wrongdoing, who misuse and abuse in his name. My mistake as an atheist was not in believing that there are hypocrites in the pews. Of course there are. My mistake was in thinking that it was up to me to figure out who they were. Jesus isn't telling me to size up my neighbor. He's warning me to size up myself.

Christianity presents us with an ideal, but it doesn't stop there. Entering into Christianity is accepting an ideal that culminates in union with a very real Person. The Christian life is one long haul to attain full communion with Jesus Christ. It's not impossible to attain it, the saints attest to that. But the fact is that it takes daily, hourly, even minute-by-minute work? That's the surprise. It is also, paradoxically, the invigorating joy of the Christian life.

St. Francis de Sales saw this dichotomy when he said:

> You recognize thousands of imperfections and failings in yourself, contrary to your desire for purity and perfect love of God. In reply I say that it is not possible to avoid all of these. While we live on this earth, we have to put up with ourselves, until the day that God takes us to heaven. Meanwhile, we can do no more than to keep a close watch on ourselves, and be patient. How can we correct in one day defects that we have contracted by our prolonged lack of diligence? Sometimes God has healed a person in an instant, without leaving a trace of his previous spiritual sickness. But in so many others he has left the scars of their conversion, for the greater benefit of their souls.[48]

The scars of my conversion serve me well, reminding me that I am a poor sinner in need of redemption. I put up with a flawed pilgrim Church because I put up with myself.

The Message That Saves

"Living with a dog," the writer H. L. Mencken reportedly said, "is messy. Like living with an idealist." And, I would add, like living with a Christian.

The pilgrim Church, the body of believers living on earth, is a ragtag bunch. Sure, we've got a central organization, complete with a hierarchy, rules, and regulations, but let's face it: we're puny. We live in a world of disease, corruption, violence, and cruelty. We are faced with conditions that, no matter how much we love the Lord, can lead us to have doubts and dark nights. We do our skeptical, unbelieving friends, and ourselves, a big favor when we simply admit that being in possession of the Catholic faith does not mean we automatically travel a smoothly paved road.

When my friend Renee was in college she got involved with a group of Catholics who told her that faith was most fully lived when we "just turn everything over to Jesus" every day. With her new friends' assurance that such daily, vocal, positive proclamations would prevent anything bad from happening, Renee was shattered when, just a few months after falling in with these friends, her mother succumbed to a tragic, debilitating depression and committed suicide. Though her friends had sincerely believed they were helping Renee, their simplistic approach to faith left her struggling with trust in God for years. "I haven't," she said, "turned anything over since without claw marks on it."

Other encounters with the pilgrim Church led to more pain. Seeking emotional and spiritual help in the aftermath of sexual abuse in childhood by a relative, Renee sought the advice and counsel of a priest. Instead of helping her find the healing she desperately needed, the priest she spoke to implied that Renee needed to grow up and move on. When the sexual abuse scandal broke, Renee, who'd been a journalist for fifteen years, chose at one point to discontinue her reporting—it was painful on so many levels. Still dealing with the residual pain of her own abuse and the priest's doltish advice, she even stepped away from her writing altogether for a short period.

Renee still battles the depression and anxiety that beset her early in life, but her toughest moment came when her fragile emotional state left her thinking she had lost all belief in God. She wrote about the experience in *Portland* magazine:

> It is one thing to think that God doesn't hear your prayers or has shifted off your radar for awhile; it is quite another to think he does not exist. After trying to figure it out by myself for a few days, I made an emergency visit to my psychiatrist, running through a box of tissues in less than ten minutes. He appeared confused—I'd been fine two months ago when he'd last seen me. What, he asked, had happened?

> "I'm not sure," I sobbed, "but I don't think I believe in God anymore."

> The hint of a smile shone in his eyes and he did something uncharacteristic: he let his soul out, overruling his by-the-book doctor persona. "That's okay," he said, leaning forward in his chair, elbows on desk, staring at my tear-streaked face and runny nose, "because God believes in you."

> God believes in you, I would tell myself on my daily walk. God believes in you, I would say as I sat in church. God

believes in you, I would repeat over and over in the shower on days I thought I simply could not go on. And, slowly, it worked.

... Perhaps, I think, what separates the faithful who thrive in spite of challenging mental conditions from those who don't is not doctors and medicine, although both are often necessary, not a Pollyannaish "faith heals" attitude toward a sometimes life-threatening condition. Perhaps what separates "thriving with depression" from "surviving depression" is a simple shift of focus, a tiny but persistent effort to see life—even a life of suffering—as gift, and then remembering that the Giver believes in you. For me, that is the message that saves.

Renee reminds me of Garrison Keillor's friend, and of my parents, of my friends, of Imogene Herdman and me, of millions of people in kind, decent, households across this country and around the world. There's evidence that God believes in every one of us. Perhaps we're all called to believe in the mystery of possibility, too, called to share the good news that even though the pilgrim Church is not a magical kingdom that will cure all our earthly ills, it's the best thing we've got. And in spite of everything, it's actually a pretty remarkable place to land, the closest thing to a home we'll find until we really make it home.

The flaws, bad behavior, scandal, sins, mistakes, and foolishness of the pilgrim Church will always be with us. Pretending otherwise does not help our cause. When will I realize that the best way to make the Church on earth a place more people want to be is to start with ... *me*?

There are a thousand things wrong with the world, the Church, and the people I am tempted to complain about. Ultimately, the best and only thing I can do is start in my own house, living the Gospel. One moment at a time, fueled by the Eucharist, with regular visits to the confessional, I remind myself that I am here to live a life of good news, which, as St. Augustine said, is simply this: "Wake up, O man! For your sake God became man!"[49]

When I remember that earth-shattering and humbling fact, I stop worrying about the pilgrim Church and get busy being part of it: Doing corporal and spiritual works of mercy. Loving my family. Giving to the poor. Learning my faith. Living it. Sharing it.

"I never look at the masses as my responsibility," said Mother Teresa. "I can only love one person at a time. I can only feed one person at a time. Just one, one, one. You get closer to Christ by coming closer to each other."[50]

Disheveled, distracted, hungry, in need of redemption ... here comes everybody.

But don't worry. It's not daunting. Just reach out. There's someone standing right next to you.

Acknowledgments

I AM ENORMOUSLY GRATEFUL to all who have shared their stories and their lives with me, especially my amazing husband, Tom, Jack and Holly Donnelly, Loretta Donnelly, Fr. Joe Taphorn, Fr. Scott Hastings, Danae and Karl Henkel, Jen and Demetrio Aguila, Renee Schafer Horton, and the many others who go unnamed or who shared their stories under pseudonyms. All the stories are true, though some details have been changed in some cases to protect the privacy of those involved. Some conversations have been reconstructed from journals and shared memories, again, with some details changed for the sake of privacy, but the original spirit of each conversation and incident remains intact.

Thank you also to Julie Davis for the serendipitous inclusion on her blog of the quote from Dickens at just the moment when I was looking for such a thing. Thanks to Brian Doyle for allowing me to quote from *Portland* Magazine. Fr. Scott, Fr. Andrews, and Fr. Niggemeyer, thanks for weighing in on a theological question. A special thank you, as always, to my tireless editor, Cindy Cavnar (who puts up with my excessive parenthetical comments and urges me to stop clinging to tired word choices), for encouraging me to write another book.

Endnotes

1 "God Chooses the Little Ones," *L'Osservatore Romano*, January 24, 2014, http://m.vatican.va/content/francescomobile/en/cotidie/2014/documents/papa-francesco-cotidie_20140121_little-ones.html.

2 "Pope Francis: The Holy Spirit opens our hearts to the world," *News.va*, May 6, 2013, http://www.news.va/en/news/pope-francis-the-holy-spirit-opens-our-hearts-to-t.

3 Henry Wadsworth Longfellow, *Hyperion, Book III, Chapter IV*, http://www.gutenberg.org/files/5436/5436-h/5436-h.htm#3_5.

4 Junno Arocho Esteves, "Pope Francis: Be unsettled because the love of Jesus is worth it," *Zenit.org*, August 14, 2013, http://www.zenit.org/en/articles/pope-francis-be-unsettled-because-the-love-of-jesus-is-worth-it.

5 "Jesus' cross invites us to be smitten by his love, Pope says," *Catholic News Agency*, July 26, 2013, http://www.catholicnewsagency.com/news/jesus-cross-invites-us-to-be-smitten-by-his-love-pope-says/.

6 Phillip Schaff, *The Confessions and Letters of St. Augustine with a Sketch of his Life and Work*, Christian Classics Ethereal Library, www.ccel.org, http://www.ccel.org/ccel/schaff/npnf101.vi.VIII.IV.html?highlight=stir,us#highlight.

7 Pope Francis, *Evangelii Gaudium* (2013), 266, http://w2.vatican.va/content/francesco/en/apost_exhortations/documents/papa-francesco_esortazione-ap_20131124_evangelii-gaudium.html#Personal_encounter_with_the_saving_love_of_Jesus.

8 G. K. Chesterton, *St. Francis of Assisi,* 7, https://books.google.com/books?id=aeh5gklAt30C&printsec=frontcover&dq=isbn:1598562827&hl=en&sa=X&ved=0CB0Q6AEwAGoVChMIh4f-i_voyAIVBOomCh3N4gML#v=onepage&q&f=false.

9 St. Bernard of Clairvaux, "Readings for the feast of St. Bernard," www.liturgies.net, http://www.liturgies.net/saints/bernard/readings.htm.

10 "Pope Francis: Church is a love story," April 24, 2013, *News.va,* http://www.news.va/en/news/pope-francis-church-is-in-a-love-story.

11 *Catechism of the Catholic Church* (Vatican, Italy: Libreria Editrice Vaticana, 2000), 45, http://www.vatican.va/archive/ccc_css/archive/catechism/p1s1c1.htm.

12 J. D. Salinger, *The Catcher in the Rye* (Boston: Little, Brown and Co., 1991), 146-47.

13 "Saint of the Day, November 20, St. Rose Philippine Duchesne," *AmericanCatholic.org,* http://www.americancatholic.org/features/saints/saint.aspx?id=1205.

14 Andrew Murray, "School of Obedience," *Christian Classics Ethereal Library,* http://www.ccel.org/ccel/murray/obedience.

15 Ibid.

16 C. S. Lewis, *Letters to Malcolm: Chiefly on Prayer: Reflections on the Intimate Dialogue between Man and God* (San Diego: Harcourt, 1992), 103-104.

17 Barbara Robinson, *The Best Christmas Pageant Ever* (New York: Harper & Row, 1988), 77.

[18] Willa Cather, *O Pioneers* (Boston: Houghton Mifflin, 1995), 70.

[19] Pope John Paul II, "Letter to Artists," 1999, 6, http://w2.vatican.va/content/john-paul-ii/en/letters/1999/documents/hf_jp-ii_let_23041999_artists.html.

[20] Franz Werfel, *Song of Bernadette* (San Francisco: Ignatius Press, 2006), 3.

[21] "Letter to Artists," 10.

[22] Aldous Huxley, *Brave New World* (New York: Harper Perennial, 1998), 11-12.

[23] *Letters of Charles Dickens to Wilkie Collins*, http://www.gutenberg.org/files/25853/25853-h/25853-h.htm.

[24] "Pope at Mass: Culture of encounter is the foundation of peace," May 22, 2013, *Radiovaticana.va*, http://en.radiovaticana.va/storico/2013/05/22/pope_at_mass_culture_of_encounter_is_the_foundation_of_peace/en1-694445.

[25] Francis Thompson, *The Hound of Heaven*, Project Gutenberg, http://www.gutenberg.org/files/30730/30730-h/30730-h.htm.

[26] George MacDonald, *Unspoken Sermons*, Project Gutenberg, http://www.gutenberg.org/cache/epub/9057/pg9057-images.html.

[27] C. S. Lewis, *The Inspirational Writings of C. S. Lewis* (New York: Inspirational Press, 1987), 100.

[28] Patricia A. McEachern, *A Holy Life: The Writings of Saint Bernadette of Lourdes* (San Francisco: Ignatius Press, 2005), 34.

29 Oblates of St. Francis De Sales Wilmington Philadelphia Province, "Daily With De Sales August 9," *www.oblates.org*, http://www.oblates.org/dss/daily_with_desales/august.php.

30 "August 14, 2012, St. Maximillian Mary Kolbe, Priest, Martyr (Memorial)," EWTN.com, http://www.ewtn.com/Devotionals/inspiration_08aug2012.asp.

31 C. S. Lewis, *The Problem of Pain* (New York: Macmillan, 1962), 93.

32 Pope John Paul II, Angelus, March 29, 1998, http://w2.vatican.va/content/john-paul-ii/en/angelus/1998/documents/hf_jp-ii_ang_29031998.html.

33 Pope Benedict XVI, Homily, March 25, 2007, http://w2.vatican.va/content/benedict-xvi/en/homilies/2007/documents/hf_ben-xvi_hom_20070325_visita-parrocchia.html.

34 Madeleine L'Engle, *A Circle of Quiet* (San Francisco: Harper & Row, 1972), 195.

35 Thomas Merton, *The Seven Storey Mountain* (New York: Harcourt Brace, 1998), 124-25.

36 George MacDonald, "Life," The Literature Network: Online Classic Literature, Poems, and Quotes. Essays & Summaries, http://www.online-literature.com/george-macdonald/3670/.

37 Pope Benedict XVI, *Deus Caritas Est* (2005), 1.

38 Pope Benedict XVI, General Audience, September 3, 2008, http://w2.vatican.va/content/benedict-xvi/en/audiences/2008/documents/hf_ben-xvi_aud_20080903.html.

[39] "Pope Encourages Personal Relationship With Christ," *Zenit. org,* October 21, 2009, http://www.zenit.org/en/articles/pope-encourages-personal-relationship-with-christ.

[40] Pope John Paul II, *Redemptoris Missio* (1990), 46, http://w2.vatican.va/content/john-paul-ii/en/encyclicals/documents/hf_jp-ii_enc_07121990_redemptoris-missio.html.

[41] Carole Brown, "The Problem with 'Not' Having a Personal Relationship with Jesus," *Homiletic Pastoral Review,* August 11, 2014, http://www.hprweb.com/2014/08/the-problem-with-not-having-a-personal-relationship-with-jesus/#fn-10929-5.

[42] *Evangelii Gaudium,* 266, http://w2.vatican.va/content/francesco/en/apost_exhortations/documents/papa-francesco_esortazione-ap_20131124_evangelii-gaudium.html.

[43] St. Francis De Sales, *www.brainyquote.com,* http://www.brainyquote.com/quotes/quotes/s/saintfranc193304.html.

[44] G. K. Chesterton, *The Well and the Shallows* (London: Parchment Books, Aziloth Books, 2012), 80.

[45] Henry David Thoreau and Jeffrey S. Cramer, *Walden: A Fully Annotated Edition* (New Haven: Yale University Press, 2004), 88.

[46] Jim Berg, "Book Review: *Orthodoxy* by G. K. Chesterton," Gel Blog, http://kbproweb.com/gel/mbookr/christculture/orthodoxy.shtml.

[47] "Saint Peter of Alcantara," *CatholicSaints.Info,* September 27, 2008, http://catholicsaints.info/saint-peter-of-alcantara/.

[48] Oblates of St. Francis De Sales Wilmington Philadelphia Province, "Daily With De Sales April 25," *www.oblates.org,* http://www.oblates.org/dss/daily_with_desales/april.php.

[49] Pope Benedict XVI, *Urbi et Orbi* Message 2005, http://w2.vatican.va/content/benedict-xvi/en/messages/urbi/documents/hf_ben-xvi_mes_20051225_urbi.html.

[50] Christie R. Ritter, *Mother Teresa: Humanitarian and Advocate for the Poor* (Edina, Minnesota: Abdo Publishing, 2011), 51.